Pack Your Bags --
JESUS
IS
COMING!

The Return of Christ,
A Discussion Manual for The American Student

BY DAWSON McALLISTER
With Clark Albright

Editorial Assistant: **Ed Wichern**
Editor and Publication Director: **Wayne Peterson**
Illustrator: **Jay B. Johnson**
Cover Photo: **David Edmonson**

SHEPHERD MINISTRIES
2845 W. Airport Freeway, Suite 137
Irving, Texas 75062
(214) 570-7599

Dawson McAllister

Dawson McAllister is one of America's outstanding youth communicators. He has been a youth pastor, coffee house counselor, author, TV and radio host and friend to thousands of teenagers.

After academic study at Bethel College in Minnesota and Talbot Theological Seminary in California, Dawson became involved in a program for runaways and desperate teenagers that has developed into a nation-wide ministry. His practical experience and spiritual insight make him much in demand as a speaker at assemblies, weekend seminars, conferences and camps. With twenty-five years of ministry to the American student, he was recently awarded an honorary doctorate of ministry degree from Biola University - Talbot Seminary.

A series of prime time TV specials entitled "Kids in Crisis" has enabled him to provide spiritual counsel to teenage youth throughout the nation. And now, an ongoing tool to reach the American teenager is live call-in radio entitled, *Dawson McAllister...Live!* This two-hour weekly satellite program brings troubled, confused teenagers into contact with straight talk and clear Biblical guidance.

Sixteen popular discussion manuals, thirteen video programs and a film series have multiplied his ministry to individuals and small groups.

Dawson lives with his wife and two sons on an historic farm outside of Nashville, Tennessee, where he enjoys breaking and training horses in his spare time.

Clark Albright

Clark Albright is a counselor, youth communicator, and Director of Research for *Dawson McAllister...Live!*, the weekly call-in talk show for teenagers.

It is Clark's vision to make Christ clear to teens and to show Him for who He really is: 'the Way, the Truth, and the Life.' Because of Clark's vision and desire for teens he works alongside Dawson assisting him in various projects.

Clark has degrees from Colorado Christian University in Biblical Studies, Youth Ministries, and Psychology. Presently he is pursuing a masters degree in counseling. He lives with his wife, Sally, and their three children in Columbia, Tennessee.

A Discussion Manual For Teenagers

Pack Your Bags — Jesus Is Coming!

Contents

Use Of This Manual

PACK YOUR BAGS — JESUS IS COMING! is a study and discussion tool for individuals, one-on-one counseling, youth groups, weekend conferences, seminars and week-long camps.

PACK YOUR BAGS — JESUS IS COMING! is a teaching manual to challenge the thinking student who is looking for answers. It is an excellent resource for the youth leader who is seeking to develop the faith and commitment of students.

Scripture passages in this manual are highlighted to call attention to their importance and to make them stand out from the context. The Bible is our ultimate resource in life and is the heart of this study. Various versions are used to bring out the vital teaching of each passage and to communicate clearly what God says!

The questions are designed to motivate thoughtful discussion, make significant points clearly understandable and to apply Scripture to the individual in current experience.

The planned progression of this study makes it important for the youth leader and the student to follow the chapter topics in succession, at least for the first time.

Introduction

In our world today, there is so much that frightens us. For example, all around us you can see:

- Tremendous hatred and lawlessness of man towards his fellow man
- Civil and international wars along with fears of a nuclear holocaust
- Natural disasters of unparalleled destruction
- The terrifying reality that tens of thousands of people die every day from disease and hunger.

It doesn't take us long to realize that something strange is happening to this world. The reality is that we are part of a world that has turned its back on God and will one day be handed over to the most evil man who will ever live—the Antichrist. Satan's dream to take over this world and be worshipped as God will turn our world into a nightmare. This period will be worse than all the terrors of history combined. This violent and deadly struggle between God's kingdom and Satan's kingdom will end in the bloodiest battle of history, and the Second Coming of Jesus Christ to reign.

In our world today, people are desperate. We want purpose and meaning in life. We want security. We want peace. We want a reason to live. We want hope.

God loves us and does not want us to go through life hopeless. The only hope for us and the people of the world is the future Return of Jesus Christ. Jesus Himself gives us promises of His Return. Christ gives us these promises—not to fill our heads with knowledge. He gives them to us to change our hearts and lives. They are to give us hope, meaning, and purpose for our lives. Living in light of His Return motivates us to be ready and alert. Any moment now Christ could sound His trumpet and come to take us from this troubled world to spend eternity with Him.

Pack your Bags—Jesus is Coming!

Let's Be Alert and Ready

1 | Let's Be Alert and Ready

There seems to be something going on in our world. Something stirring. Something bothersome. Things just don't seem to hold together like they once did.

- Violence around the world and in our schools and in our cities and even our homes seems to be increasing and no one seems to be able to stop it.

- Diseases are sweeping the world and there seems to be no way to cure them.

- World economies seem shakier than ever before with each country's economy depending on another.

- There are more natural disasters than anyone can remember in the past. More famines, more earthquakes, more environmental disasters.

- And there is a serious moral decline all around us. It's almost as though people don't know or don't care what Christian values are.

There is a sense that the problems of this world, no matter how much we talk about them or how much we do with our technological breakthroughs, are unsolvable.

Are you ever concerned with what's going on in our troubled world? Why?

_____

_____

_____

1 | Let's Be Alert and Ready

What is it that's happening around the world which troubles you most?

_____

_____

_____

Our troubled world causes us to ask some difficult but exciting questions:

- Could we be coming to the end of the world?
- Could we be near the time the Bible calls the 'end of the age?'
- Could the final war, the Battle of Armageddon, be on the horizon?
- Is this generation of high school students the last before the Return of Christ?
- Could Jesus Christ return to earth any moment now?

How much do you know about the end of the world? Most Christian students know very little about the Return of Christ. They don't seem to understand that Jesus could return at any moment. Therefore, they fail to obey Christ's command to His disciples. In Mark 13, Jesus spoke to His disciples about His return:

Mark 13:32-33; 37 (NIV)
32) "No one knows about that day or hour, not even the angels in heaven, nor the Son, but only the Father.
33) Be on guard! Be alert! You do not know when that time will come.....
37) What I say to you, I say to everyone: 'Watch!'"

Let's Be Alert and Ready | 1

According to Mark 13:32-33 and 37, what commands does Jesus give His followers?

_____

_____

_____

_____

It is time for Christian students to begin to watch for the Return of Christ. It is time that we realize that this generation may be the last generation, the one that witnesses the Return of Jesus Christ; we need to change our lives accordingly.

> # IN THIS CHAPTER WE WILL CONSIDER SOME OF THE REASONS WHY THE RETURN OF CHRIST IS INCREDIBLY IMPORTANT TO CHRISTIAN STUDENTS.

I. THE RETURN OF JESUS CHRIST IS INCREDIBLY IMPORTANT TO US BECAUSE JESUS COMMANDS US TO BE WATCHFUL AND READY FOR HIS RETURN.

As we look in the Bible, we find that God takes seriously the Return of His son Jesus Christ to this earth. In the Old Testament at least half of the many prophecies pertaining to Jesus Christ relate to His Return and rule on this earth. When we look in the New Testament, we see that up to 319 verses, or 1 out of every 25 verses is devoted to the Return of Jesus Christ. Jesus himself commanded his disciples to take very seriously His Return. He said in Matthew 24:42-44 —

Matthew 24:42-44 (NIV)
42) "Therefore keep watch, because you do not know on what day your Lord will come.
43) But understand this: if the owner of the house had known at what time of night the thief was coming, he would have kept watch and would not have let his house be broken into.
44) So you also must be ready, because the Son of Man will come at an hour when you do not expect him."

1 Let's Be Alert and Ready

Jesus commanded His disciples in Matthew 24:42-44 'to keep watch.' What do you think 'keep watch' means?

_____

_____

_____

Jesus makes it clear that we as Christians do not know on what day He will come. Why is it that God has kept secret the timing of the Return of Christ?

_____

_____

_____

Because we have a human nature, we could easily become indifferent and lazy. If we knew the exact time of Christ's Return, we might ignore preparations for it until the very last moment. Christians would quickly lose the cutting edge of their faith and turn to indifference and laziness. Since we don't know the time of His Return, we must be constantly ready and alert at all times.

How do you think we as Christians can be ready?

_____

_____

_____

Let's Be Alert and Ready | 1

It is obvious that the focus of the Christian is to live his or her life with the anticipation of Christ returning at any moment. Jesus made it clear that if we are truly His disciples we will be watchful and ready for His Return. When Jesus gave these powerful commands to His disciples, He was not only telling the followers of His day to obey. Jesus commands all Christians everywhere to watch for His Return. He said in Mark 13:37 —

> Mark 13:37 (NIV)
> *"What I say to you, I say to everyone: 'Watch!'"*

PROJECT:

- Quote the above verse, but add your name:
  "What I say to you, I say to _____: 'Watch!'"
- Think about that verse every day this week. What changes would take place in your life if you followed this command?

_____

_____

_____

_____

1 Let's Be Alert and Ready

II. THE RETURN OF JESUS CHRIST IS INCREDIBLY IMPORTANT TO US BECAUSE UNDERSTANDING THE FUTURE GIVES MEANING TO OUR LIFE IN THE PRESENT.

Students who do not know Jesus Christ and Christian students who do not understand the future find themselves living only for the 'nothingness' of today. It is almost as though the only things that govern our lives are the happenings of today. What clothes we should wear, what car we should drive, what party we should go to... all for today. But after awhile our shallow lives of living for today leave us empty, apathetic, with purposelessness as our only compass. The Bible talks about people who live for today in Isaiah 22:13 —

Isaiah 22:13 (NIV)
"But see, there is joy and revelry, slaughtering of cattle and killing of sheep, eating of meat and drinking of wine! 'Let us eat and drink,' you say, 'for tomorrow we die!'"

Obviously God is concerned about the present. But our present life is affected by the past. For example, the fact that Christ died on the Cross in the past should greatly influence our lives in the present. At the same time Scripture is clear that our present life should also be profoundly impacted by what will take place in the future. God speaks about this in Hebrews 10:24-25 —

1 | Let's Be Alert and Ready

> Hebrews 10:24-25 (NIV)
> 24) "And let us consider how we may spur one another on toward love and good deeds.
> 25) Let us not give up meeting together, as some are in the habit of doing, but let us encourage one another - and all the more as you see the Day approaching."

According to Hebrews 10:24-25 what are some of the things we should be doing as Christians in our present life?

_____

_____

_____

_____

The writer of the book of Hebrews said we should do these things *and all the more as you see the Day approaching.'*

What do you think this means?

_____

_____

_____

_____

Let's Be Alert and Ready | **1**

God does not want us floating through life. There is a purpose in living and a purpose in dying. God has an eternal plan for the world and our lives. God asks all Christians to do far more than 'eat drink and be merry.' He wants our lives to be totally different from those who don't know Christ. A Christian should understand that this life is just a few short years but eternity is what really matters. And when Christ returns, eternity will begin. The Apostle Paul talks about this in Philippians 3:19,20—

Philippians 3:19-20 (NIV)
19) "Their destiny is destruction, their god is their stomach, and their glory is in their shame. Their mind is on earthly things.
20) But our citizenship is in heaven. And we eagerly await a Savior from there, the Lord Jesus Christ."

Focusing on the Return of Christ keeps our minds on the importance of eternity and how our lives should count today. We must constantly remind ourselves that we are not simply living for today; we are living for Christ and an eternity with Him.

1 | Let's Be Alert and Ready

III. *THE RETURN OF JESUS CHRIST IS INCREDIBLY IMPORTANT TO US BECAUSE KNOWING THAT CHRIST COULD RETURN AT ANY MOMENT MOTIVATES US TO LIVE HOLY LIVES.*

The Bible is clear that Christ could return at any moment. But of course no one knows the day or the hour. This much we do know: When Christ returns, we in no way want to be embarrassed by our lives when He comes.

The Bible is very clear that God wants us to be waiting, ready, and living a lifestyle that is pleasing to Christ. What better way to please Christ than to be living a holy life when He returns. The Bible talks about this in 2 Peter 3 —

> 2 Peter 3:10-12a and 14 (NIV)
> *10) "But the day of the Lord will come like a thief. The heavens will disappear with a roar; the elements will be destroyed by fire, and the earth and everything in it will be laid bare.*
> *11) Since everything will be destroyed in this way, what kind of people ought you to be? You ought to live holy and godly lives*
> *12) as you look forward to the day of God and speed its coming....*
> *14) So then, dear friends, since you are looking forward to this, make every effort to be found spotless, blameless and at peace with Him."*

1 | Let's Be Alert and Ready

According to 2 Peter 3:10, what two things do we know about the Return of Christ?

_____

_____

_____

_____

Since the time of the coming of Christ is so serious, so powerful, and so deadly, God has asked us to be a certain kind of person. What kind of people should we be?

_____

_____

_____

_____

PROJECT:

If you knew Christ was coming in the next two weeks how would your life be different?

• List some activities that you would start doing.

_____

_____

_____

_____

● List some activities that you would stop doing.

_____

_____

_____

_____

Every day we need to be able to say to ourselves: **This may be the day that Jesus comes again.** We ought to be able to arrange our entire lives around that fact. The truth that Jesus could come back any day should motivate us moment by moment to live holy lives. The Apostle John sums up in 1 John 2:28 what our lives should be like when Christ returns —

---

1 John 2:28 (NIV)
"And now, dear children, continue in him, so that when he appears we may be confident and unashamed before him at his coming."

The Bible is very clear in 1 John 2:28 that if we live a life that is pleasing to God, we will be confident and unashamed at His Return. But the opposite is also true. If we as Christians have had a lifestyle that is not disciplined or empowered by the Holy Spirit, we will be ashamed when He returns. God wants us to let the truth that Christ could return at any moment motivate us to live pure lives. The Apostle John sums up this truth very clearly when he writes in 1 John 3:2-3 —

---

1 John 3:2-3 (NIV)
2) "Dear friends, now we are children of God, and what we will be has not yet been made known. But we know that when he appears, we shall be like him, for we shall see him as he is.
3) Everyone who has this hope in him purifies himself, just as he is pure."

---

1 Let's Be Alert and Ready

IV. THE RETURN OF JESUS CHRIST IS INCREDIBLY IMPORTANT TO US BECAUSE IT GIVES EVERY CHRISTIAN HOPE.

One does not have to be a rocket scientist to figure out that the world is in a mess. First, consider the global problems we are having.

● Make a list of what you think are the greatest problems facing the world. (For example: famines, earthquakes, wars...)

_____

_____

_____

_____

Then, there are problems facing the American teenager that seem unsolvable.

● Make a list of some of those problems. (For example: depression, sexual-physical-verbal abuse, violence, drugs and alcohol...)

_____

_____

_____

_____

1 | Let's Be Alert and Ready

If we looked only at the circumstances around us we could easily be thrown into despair. There are no guarantees that things will get better. The world is a difficult place in which to live. It gives us pain and heartbreak beyond our worst nightmares. But Christians don't have to be caught in the vicious circle of fear and despair. We can look in the Bible and know how the world will end. It is in the Bible that we see that Christ will come and bring peace, joy and sanity to this world again. So while others fall apart in the Last Days, Christians can have a calm, confident hope that Christ will return and things will get much, much better. It is clear from Scripture that the realization of eternity in heaven gives our pained lives perspective and hope for today. The Bible talks about this in 2 Corinthians 4:16-18 —

---

2 Corinthians 4:16-18 (TLB)

16) "That is why we never give up. Though our bodies are dying, our inner strength in the Lord is growing every day.

17) These troubles and sufferings of ours are, after all, quite small and won't last very long. Yet this short time of distress will result in God's richest blessing upon us forever and ever!

18) So we do not look at what we can see right now, the troubles all around us, but we look forward to the joys in heaven which we have not yet seen. The troubles will soon be over, but the joys to come will last forever."

In 2 Corinthians 4:17 the Apostle Paul describes three things about our sufferings on this present earth. What are they?

_____

_____

_____

_____

Let's Be Alert and Ready | **1**

What do you think Paul meant when he said, *"Yet this short time of distress will result in God's richest blessing upon us forever and ever."*

_____

_____

_____

_____

According to 2 Corinthians 4:18, what does the Apostle Paul want us to focus on?

_____

_____

_____

_____

There is no question that there is suffering today all around us. Christians are not and will not be immune to the pain of living in a dying world. But we can have hope if we put all these sufferings and troubles into an eternal perspective. Whatever we may suffer on this earth is short in comparison to eternity. The joy that we will have with God forever will far outweigh any distress we might have as this sinful and tired world comes to a close. As we look at the dark clouds of world disorder and destruction, we can comfort our hearts with the promise of Revelation 22:20 —

> Revelation 22:20 (TLB)
> *"He who has said all these things declares: Yes I am coming soon!"*

1 | Let's Be Alert and Ready

CONCLUSION

ARE YOU READY FOR CHRIST'S RETURN?

Jesus commanded His followers to be on the alert and watch for His Return. He knew that if we would watch and be on the alert, our lives would have meaning as we worked to live a holy life. God does not want us discouraged as we come to the end of time. He wants us to have hope. And that hope is that Christ is coming for us soon. May we always be on the watch, may we always be on the alert and may we always have that hope.

2 | Warning Signs of Christ's Return

As we saw in the last chapter, God wants us to be alert and on the look-out for the Return of Jesus Christ. He does not want us ignorant or passive about Christ's return. In fact, Christ spoke very directly about Christians watching for His Return when He said in Mark 13 —

> Mark 13:37 (NIV)
> *"What I say to you, I say to everyone: 'Watch!'"*

Therefore it would be extremely wise for us to be "expert watchers" so that we are not taken by surprise at His Return.

- What are we to be watching for?
- How can we know the time when He will come?
- What can we do so we are not surprised when He appears?

The disciples must have thought the same things, so they went to Jesus and asked Him a most dramatic question, as recorded in Matthew 24:3 —

> Matthew 24:3 (NIV)
> *"As Jesus was sitting on the Mount of Olives, the disciples came to him privately. 'Tell us,' they said, 'when will this happen, and what will be the sign of your coming and of the end of the age?'"*

Jesus sat with His disciples and began to explain to them the signs that would give clear indication when He would return. Jesus does not want His disciples or us to be confused. The signs He gave are road maps that we can follow to help us understand the general time of His appearing.

IN THIS CHAPTER WE WILL LOOK AT SOME OF THE AMAZING SIGNS THAT POINT TO CHRIST'S RETURN.

Warning Signs of Christ's Return | 2

SIGN 1 *Spiritual Anarchy and Chaos*

One of the signs of the Return of Christ is that there will be at that time a great falling away from God and His truth. This massive falling away from God will lead tens of millions of people into spiritual anarchy and chaos. As the world comes to an end, Satan and his demons will have such a fear of Christ that Satan will raise up fake Christs and false prophets. Satan will work through these to confuse and lead astray as many people as possible. Jesus predicted that this great falling away would occur. For example, Jesus talks about this in Matthew 24 —

Matthew 24:4-5; 10-11; 24-26 (NIV)
4) "Jesus answered: Watch out that no one deceives you.
5) For many will come in my name, claiming, 'I am the Christ,' and will deceive many.
10) At that time many will turn away from the faith and will betray and hate each other,
11) and many false prophets will appear and deceive many people.
24) For false Christs and false prophets will appear and perform great signs and miracles to deceive even the elect - if that were possible.
25) See, I have told you ahead of time.
26) So if anyone tells you, 'There he is, out in the desert,' do not go out; or, 'Here he is, in the inner rooms,' do not believe it."

What is a false Christ?

_____

_____

_____

_____

Jesus said there would be many false Christs. These false Christs will be very deceptive. Since they are moved along by the power of Satan, they will be able to perform great signs and miracles. So powerful are these false Christs that in the end times even Christians, were it not for the grace of God, would be deceived by them.

Do you know of any false Christs today?

_____

_____

_____

_____

CHRIST ALSO SPOKE OF FALSE PROPHETS

Not only will there be counterfeit Christs in the end times, but also there will be false prophets who will be used by Satan to lead people away from God. Matthew 24:11 tells us —

> Matthew 24:11 (NIV)
> *"and many false prophets will appear and deceive many people."*

What are false prophets?

_____

_____

_____

Warning Signs of Christ's Return

A false prophet does not claim to be Christ but will powerfully proclaim a false faith that goes against God and His teachings.

While there have always been false Christs and false prophets, it would appear that as time comes to a close there will be many, many more. Millions of people will follow these false Christs because they are already under the power of Satan. Therefore they will easily believe the seductive teaching and power of false Christs and false prophets. Satan will attempt to destroy the Church at the end of time and will deceive people who are religious but do not really know Christ. Jesus tells us that Satan's work of deceiving people through false Christs and prophets will be extremely successful. Jesus said in Matthew 24:10 —

> Matthew 24:10 (NIV)
> *"At that time many will turn away from the faith and will betray and hate each other,"*

True Christians are warned not to believe in the deceptive work of false Christs and false prophets. Christ warns us in Matthew 24:26 —

> Matthew 24:26 (NIV)
> *"So if anyone tells you, 'There he is, out in the desert,' do not go out; or, 'Here he is, in the inner rooms,' do not believe it."*

Warning Signs of Christ's Return | 2

SIGN 2   *Wars and Rumors of Wars*

There is nothing new about war. Ever since Cain murdered Abel, men and nations have been fighting and killing each other. Yet, Jesus warns us that there will be an increase of war as time, as we know it, comes to an end. The hostility between nations and ethnics will increase greatly in number and intensity. Jesus spoke of the reality of wars at the end of time when He said in Matthew 24:6-7a —

> Matthew 24:6-7a (NIV)
> *6) "You will hear of wars and rumors of wars, but see to it that you are not alarmed. Such things must happen, but the end is still to come.*
> *7) Nation will rise against nation, and kingdom against kingdom."*

Why do you think Christ did not want his disciples to be frightened when they saw 'wars and rumors of war'?

_____

_____

_____

Jesus taught his disciples that warfare was not a sign of the end but only a sign of the beginning of the end. No one war is a sign of Christ's return but as wars and ethnic violence increase, they tell us that we are progressing towards that ultimate war that ends all wars: the Battle of Armageddon.

As you look around do you see more wars, rumors of wars and ethnic violence?

_____

_____

_____

Warning Signs of Christ's Return | 2

SIGN 3 *Famines and an Increase in World Hunger*

Where there is war there will be famine. Jesus warned that there would not only be wars and rumors of wars at the end of time, but famines as well. He said in Matthew 24:7b —

> Matthew 24:7b (NIV)
> *"There will be famines..."*

Mankind has always had to struggle for his food. Without doubt, there has been starvation from earliest times. Jesus seems to be implying that famines will increase as we approach the end. Throughout the world, there are plenty of resources to feed people. Yet due to war, tribal and ethnic strife and poor distribution, millions of people starve to death every year. Its hard to believe that as we enter the 21st century with all of our technological advancement, people are still starving to death. In fact, the phenomena of famine will only increase, not subside, as Christ prepares to return to this earth.

As you look at our world today, do you see famines on the increase?

_____

_____

_____

_____

SIGN 4 *Earthquakes*

Jesus predicted that there would be not only the horror of famine but the terror of earthquakes as time comes to a close. He said in Matthew 24:7b —

> Matthew 24:7b (NIV)
> *"There will be famines and earthquakes in various places."*

History tells us that the disaster of earthquakes has always been with us. In fact, the Bible predicts a final and great earthquake just before the Second Coming of Jesus Christ. Revelation 16:18 says,

> Revelation 16:18 (NIV)
> *18) "Then there came flashes of lightning, rumblings, peals of thunder and a severe earthquake. No earthquake like it has ever occurred since man has been on earth, so tremendous was the quake."*

This last earthquake will cause incredible damage and an immense loss of life. Up until the final earthquake there is no one earthquake that actually can tell us that Christ is about to return. However, with an increase in earthquakes, we seem to be moving quickly toward the last and final one before the Second Coming of Christ.

Do you think the world is experiencing more earthquakes than ever?

_____

_____

_____

_____

Warning Signs of Christ's Return

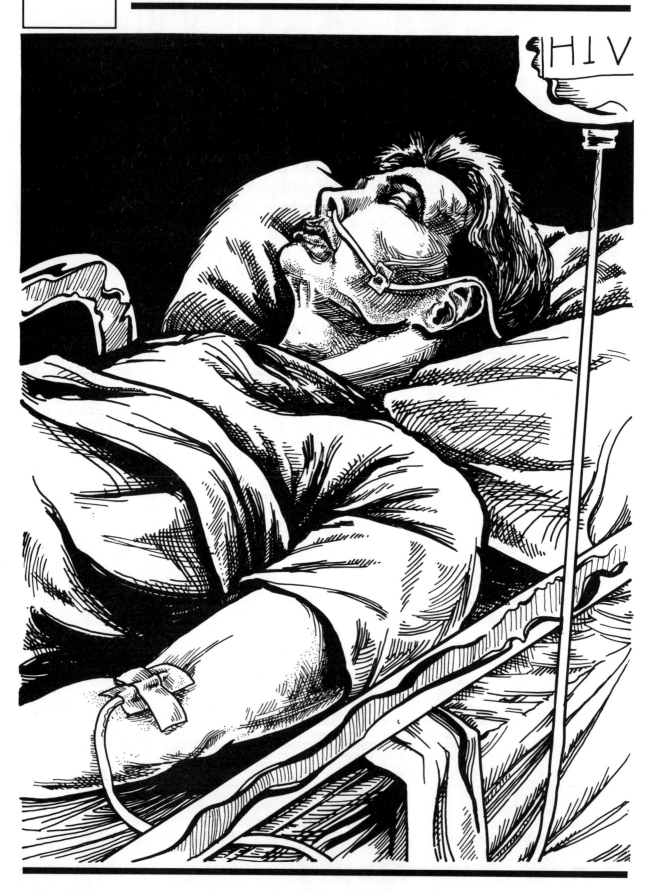

SIGN 5   *Sweeping Incurable Diseases (Pestilences & Plagues)*

Still another sign of the Return of Christ is the increasing occurrence of sweeping and incurable diseases. Jesus called these diseases, pestilences. He said in Luke 21:11 —

> Luke 21:11 (NIV)
> *"There will be great earthquakes, famines and pestilences in various places,"*

With the increase in wars and famine there will be an increase in pestilence. Modern medicine has been able to cure some plagues which in the past have wiped out entire populations. Yet new incurable diseases find themselves plaguing mankind. Because of war and ignorance and the problems of distribution, some parts of the world cannot receive medical attention to stop a spreading plague. Jesus clearly taught that as we come to the end of time we will see sweeping incurable diseases becoming more active and deadly.

Are there more incurable diseases today than ever? Can you name any?

_____

_____

_____

_____

2 | **Warning Signs of Christ's Return**

SIGN 6   *Increase of Lawlessness*

Jesus predicted that before His return the world would be on the verge of utter collapse. Many people will turn away from God. Because God is the author of law and order, when masses of people turn away from God, they are left to their own unchecked lawlessness. Jesus spoke of this lawlessness in Matthew 24:12 —

Matthew 24:12 (NASV)
"And because lawlessness is increased, most people's love will grow cold."

Who would have ever thought that 2,000 years ago, Jesus could have predicted the anarchy that is now happening within countries, states, cities, and homes of this world? The Apostle Paul also predicted that in the last days, lawlessness due to the rebellion in man's hearts will increase. He said in 2 Timothy 3:1-5 —

---

2 Timothy 3:1-5 (NIV)
1) "But mark this: There will be terrible times in the last days.
2) People will be lovers of themselves, lovers of money, boastful, proud, abusive, disobedient to their parents, ungrateful, unholy,
3) without love, unforgiving, slanderous, without self-control, brutal, not lovers of the good,
4) treacherous, rash, conceited, lovers of pleasure rather than lovers of God -
5) having a form of godliness but denying its power."

Do you see signs of lawlessness increasing in the world today? Can you name examples?

_____

_____

_____

SIGN 7 *Persecution of Christians*

The closer we come to the end of time, the more Satan understands that his great judgment is about to begin. He has come to detest anyone or anything that lives for Christ. Therefore, he will put on an all-out attack on Christians. He knows that if he can stamp out those who tell others about Christ, he will have greater power over a lost world. Satan will work behind the scenes through deceived and misled non-Christians to start a major persecution against those who believe. Jesus talked about this major persecution in Matthew 24:9 —

> Matthew 24:9 (NIV)
> *"Then you will be handed over to be persecuted and put to death, and you will be hated by all nations because of me."*

Christians have always suffered some form of persecution throughout history. Yet in the last days, the attack against Christianity will accelerate as we head towards the Return of Christ.

Is there persecution of Christians around the world today? Can you list any examples in our country, your state, city, or even school?

_____

_____

_____

SIGN 8   *Worldwide Proclamation of the Gospel*

In Matthew 24:14, Jesus made a prediction about the End Times which up until a few years ago seemed all but impossible to fulfill. The prediction was that in the end, the Good News of Jesus Christ would be preached everywhere to everyone. Jesus said in Matthew 24:14 —

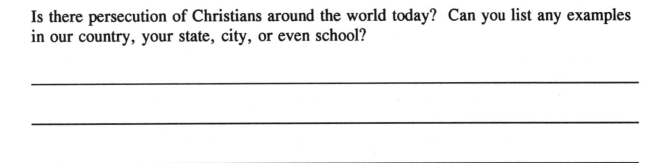

> Matthew 24:14 (NIV)
> *"And this gospel of the kingdom will be preached in the whole world as a testimony to all nations, and then the end will come."*

Two thousand years ago, Jesus made this prediction when no one knew there would be such things as radio, television, fax machines, air travel, computers, satellites, etc. And yet now as we quickly come upon the 21st century, all of these tools can be and have been used to spread the Gospel of Christ. Christ's prediction is coming true that just before His return, people everywhere would hear the Gospel.

Do you see evidence that the Gospel of Christ is being proclaimed around the world?

_____

_____

_____

SIGN 9   *Israel Is In The Land*

In Matthew 24, Jesus appeared to be speaking about something mysterious and hard to understand when he predicted:

Matthew 24:15 (NIV)
"So when you see standing in the holy place 'the abomination that causes desolation,' spoken of through the prophet Daniel - let the reader understand-"

Jesus was referring to the Great Tribulation that would take place at the end of this age. The Bible tells us that this tribulation will last seven years. Christ also referred to the book of Daniel and what he called the 'abomination of desolation.' In the book of Daniel, the Old Testament prophet predicted there would come one whom the Bible calls the Anti-Christ who would stand against God and try to rule the world for Satan. Daniel tells us this Antichrist would rule from the temple in Jerusalem. Up until 1948, the prediction seemed to be an impossibility that there would be one who would come and then rule the world from Israel. Anyone who studied history knew that there was no longer such a state of Israel. The nation of Israel and the Jews who lived in it had been scattered around the world. The Jews for two thousand years had been hated, persecuted, murdered, and found living in almost every part of the world. But in 1948 a miracle took place. Israel, against all odds, became a nation again.

Why do you think it's such a miracle that Israel is once again a nation?

_____

_____

_____

_____

CONCLUSION

There are other signs of the Return of Christ additional to those nine listed here. Other signs include: increased knowledge, difficult times, men talking of peace and security, people with exaggerated riches, etc. The point of this particular chapter should be clear: The beginning of the fulfillment of these signs is happening now! Although some of these signs will not completely come to pass until after the Rapture, they still give us clear warning that the end is coming.

All the things that need to happen before the Return of Christ have come about. There is nothing to stop Christ from returning at any moment. In Luke 21:28 Jesus made clear to his disciples what our response should be as we see the signs begin to happen.

> Luke 21:28 (NCV)
> *"When these things begin to happen, look up and hold your heads high, because the time when God will free you is near!"*

As we see the coming signs of His near return our response is simple. We should watch for Him and live a life that is pleasing to Him in every way. We should be able to say what John said in Revelation 22:20 —

> Revelation 22:20 (NASV)
> *"He who testifies to these things says, 'Yes, I am coming quickly.' Amen. Come, Lord Jesus."*

Are you ready for Christ's Return?

10…

9…

8…

7…

6…

5…

4…

3…

2…

3 The Rapture

As we saw in the last chapter, the signs that the Bible talked about which point to the Return of Jesus Christ are now happening. It would seem that soon the next great event in the history of the world will take place. When this great event happens it will not be simply one of the greatest moments in history, but also the fulfillment of a promise that Jesus made to His followers nearly 2,000 years ago. He said in John 14:1-3 —

John 14:1-3 (NIV)
1) "Do not let your hearts be troubled. Trust in God; trust also in me.
2) In my Father's house are many rooms; if it were not so, I would have told you. I am going there to prepare a place for you.
3) And if I go and prepare a place for you, I will come back and take you to be with me that you also may be where I am."

According to John 14:2-3, Christ promised his disciples that he would perform two incredible tasks for them. What were they?

_____

_____

_____

_____

Jesus said in John 14:3 *"I will come back and take you to be with me that you also may be where I am."* What do you think that promise means?

_____

_____

_____

_____

Jesus always says what He means and keeps every promise. He not only promised to prepare a place for us to live for eternity but also promised to come back to this earth and to receive His followers. That great event in time when Christ will come back and take His followers to be with Him has a special name:

IN THIS CHAPTER WE WILL DISCUSS CHRIST'S RETURN FOR HIS FOLLOWERS, KNOWN ALSO AS THE 'RAPTURE'

3 | The Rapture

The Rapture | 3

I. UNDERSTANDING THE MEANING OF THE WORD 'RAPTURE'

The word 'rapture' is often used by Christians in the discussion of the return of Christ. However, that word is never mentioned in the Bible. The word 'rapture' is a word taken from a phrase mentioned in 1 Thessalonians 4. It says,

---

1 Thessalonians 4:17 (NIV)
"After that, we who are still alive and are left will be caught up together with them in the clouds to meet the Lord in the air. And so we will be with the Lord forever."

The word 'rapture' describes the phrase in 1 Thessalonians 4:17 "to be caught up.' The Greek verb here means 'to gather up' or 'to seize, to grasp, to snatch up forcibly.' 1 Thessalonians 4:17 tells us that Christ will return and 'gather up' or 'snatch up' (or rapture) all believers. This 'gathering up' will be a miraculous moment in history where Christians will be supernaturally removed and transferred from earth into heaven. When the 'Rapture' occurs it will be one of the greatest moments in eternity.

II. UNDERSTANDING WHAT WILL TAKE PLACE AT THE RAPTURE.

The Rapture itself is an incredible event. It will only happen once in history. When it happens it will be the beginning of the end of time as we know it. Although the Rapture will take place with incredible speed, it will be a moment of beauty and power to be remembered for eternity. Even though the Rapture itself will happen quickly, the Bible tells us how the sequence of the events will unfold. There is no clearer Scripture that describes what will happen at the Rapture than 1 Thessalonians 4:16-18 —

---

1 Thessalonians 4:16-18 (NIV)

16) "For the Lord himself will come down from heaven, with a loud command, with the voice of the archangel and with the trumpet call of God, and the dead in Christ will rise first.

17) After that, we who are still alive and are left will be caught up together with them in the clouds to meet the Lord in the air. And so we will be with the Lord forever .

18) Therefore encourage each other with these words. "

3 | The Rapture

A. DURING THE RAPTURE, CHRIST WILL APPEAR IN THE AIR.

It is clear in 1 Thessalonians 4:16a that Jesus Christ Himself will appear. The Bible says,

> 1 Thessalonians 4:16a (NIV)
> *"For the Lord himself will come down from heaven,"*

Why do you think Christ Himself will personally come down from heaven to gather up the Christians and bring them to himself?

_____

_____

_____

_____

At the time of the Rapture, Jesus Christ will have one thing in mind: to gather up both those dead and alive who have believed in Him. Like a bridegroom who comes for his bride, or the father looking for his son, Christ Himself will come to gather up His followers. There is no way that Jesus would delegate that task to anyone else. He promised to come for us to welcome us to Himself. When He comes, it will be out of great respect and love for those of us who have believed in Him.

CHRIST'S LOVE AND RESPECT SHOWN FOR STEPHEN

Christ's love and respect for those who believe in Him can been demonstrated from the Bible. In Acts chapter 7 there is an amazing story about a man named Stephen. Stephen loved Christ deeply and was bold in telling others about Jesus. The Bible tells us that he was preaching to a large crowd of people who were hostile about Jesus. This crowd became so vicious and angry at Stephen, they stoned him to death. Just before his stoning, Stephen saw something truly amazing:

Acts 7:54-56 (NIV)
54) "When they heard this, they were furious and gnashed their teeth at him.
55) But Stephen, full of the Holy Spirit, looked up to heaven and saw the glory of God, and Jesus standing at the right hand of God.
56) 'Look,' he said, 'I see heaven open and the Son of Man standing at the right hand of God!"

What did Stephen see as he looked into the heavens?

_____

_____

_____

Stephen saw Jesus standing at the right hand of God. Yet the Bible seems to describe Jesus as normally sitting at the right hand of God. Evidently Jesus was so moved because of Stephen's love for Him that He stood to receive him as he came into eternity. Christ will not simply stand to receive His followers at the time of the Rapture. He will come down from heaven to meet them in the air. What a thrilling moment that will be for all the Christians who are alive at that moment.

3 | The Rapture

B. DURING THE RAPTURE, THERE WILL BE SOME KIND OF HEAVENLY SONIC BOOM.

When the Rapture takes place the Bible tells us that three unique sounds will come together and fill the air.

> 1 Thessalonians 4:16 (NIV)
> *"For the Lord himself will come down from heaven, with a loud command, with the voice of the archangel and with the trumpet call of God...."*

According to 1 Thessalonians 4:16 there will be three unique sounds when Christ returns for His people. What are those sounds?

_____

_____

_____

_____

_____

3 | The Rapture

1. At the Rapture a Voice will come down from Heaven with a Loud Command.

The Rapture will begin with a loud command from Jesus Himself, much like a powerful commander shouting the command of 'charge' to his soldiers. So shall there be a powerful command from Jesus Christ. There is tremendous power when Jesus makes a loud command. We know that in John 11:43, Jesus commanded Lazarus to come forth from the dead. So powerful was that command that it brought life back to a dead man. And so at this climatic time in history with great authority and urgency and with lightning-swift speed, Christ will command heaven and earth to meet in the air.

2. At the Rapture there will be the Sound of the Voice of the Archangel.

The Bible tells us that Jesus Christ will not be the only one to appear at the Rapture. He will appear with the voice of an archangel. An archangel is an angel who is top angel over tens of thousands of other angels in heaven. There is only one archangel listed in the Bible and his name is Michael (Jude 9). Whatever archangel or angels appear with Jesus, they too will be making some kind of heavenly angelic sound at the Rapture.

The Rapture | 3

3. At the Rapture there will be the Sound of the Trumpet of God.

In both Old and New Testament, trumpets were used as a signal that something special was about to take place. In Old Testament times, trumpets were associated with some kind of activity from God (Exodus 19:16). In Roman times, trumpets were used to announce the arrival of a great person. And in the New Testament, trumpets are a signal that Christ is about to appear. As we all know, the sound of a trumpet is so sharp and distinct that it always gets people's attention with its blast. At the time of the Rapture, the trumpet will announce that God is moving and a great person has arrived. That person is none other than Jesus Christ.

WHAT A SOUND THAT WILL BE!

There has never been a sound quite like the sound that will be heard at the time of the Rapture. Three great sounds will come together in some kind of heavenly boom. Christ's Holy Command, the mighty voice of the archangel, and the heavenly blast of a trumpet will announce that something awesome is taking place. That event is none other than the Great Rapture.

3 The Rapture

C. AT THE TIME OF THE RAPTURE, THE DEAD IN CHRIST SHALL RISE FIRST.

When Christ appears for His saints it will be a one-of-a-kind moment. Seemingly, there will be so much happening in the spiritual realm it's hard for our small minds to comprehend it. Nevertheless, the Bible tells us that something incredible will take place at the Rapture. The Bible tells us:

---

1 Thessalonians 4:16 (NIV)
"For the Lord himself will come down from heaven, with a loud command, with the voice of the archangel and with the trumpet call of God, and the dead in Christ will rise first."

Who do you think the 'dead in Christ' are?

_____

_____

_____

_____

_____

3 | The Rapture

Paul tells us that the first people to meet Christ in the air are those people who have put their faith in Christ but have physically died. It is obvious that we are talking about millions of people whose bodies will meet up with their souls in a new spiritual body that God has designed for us for eternity. When a person dies, the Bible tells us that two things happen. The body goes to the grave, and remains on this earth. But the soul of the person, the spiritual part of him, goes on to be with Christ. Somehow at the Rapture, the physical bodies of those who have died will be transformed into a new bodies that will last forever: new 'resurrection bodies'. In 1 Corinthians 15:50-53, the Bible helps us to more clearly understand this transformation.

---

1 Corinthians 15:50-53 (TLB)

50) "I tell you this, my brothers: an earthly body made of flesh and blood cannot get into God's Kingdom. These perishable bodies of ours are not the right kind to live forever.

51) But I am telling you this strange and wonderful secret: we shall not all die, but we shall all be given new bodies!

52) It will all happen in a moment, in the twinkling of an eye, when the last trumpet is blown. For there will be a trumpet blast from the sky, and all the Christians who have died will suddenly become alive, with new bodies that will never, never die; and then we who are still alive shall suddenly have new bodies too.

53) For our earthly bodies, the ones we have now that can die, must be transformed into heavenly bodies that cannot perish but will live forever."

Our small finite minds can never comprehend how God will cause the soul of a Christian who has died to join up with their new 'Resurrection' body at the time of the Rapture. But God is a big God who can create and redesign in less time than it takes for our eyes to blink. God is going to show His greatness at one of the most spectacular events in the history of eternity — the Rapture.

D. **AT THE TIME OF THE RAPTURE, CHRISTIANS WHO ARE STILL ALIVE WILL BE CAUGHT UP IN THE AIR TO MEET CHRIST AND BE WITH HIM FOREVER.**

When we think of the Rapture it is easy to forget about the heavenly sonic boom and the fact that the dead in Christ will rise first. But just about every Christian thinks about the moment he or she will be snatched instantly from the realm of this earth into the realm of the heavenly. Paul talks about this in 1 Thessalonians 4:17 —

1 Thessalonians 4:17 (NIV)
"After that, we who are still alive and are left will be caught up together with them in the clouds to meet the Lord in the air. And so we will be with the Lord forever."

As we have already seen, in the time it takes to blink an eye, Christians will be supernaturally removed from this earth. Those believers who are alive on this earth will join in the air all of the believers who have already died in Christ. Like those who have gone before us, we, too will be given 'Resurrection' bodies. In an instant our old, frail, decaying body with all it's weaknesses will be transformed into a body like the body of Jesus Christ. We will find ourselves surrounded by tens of millions of people who love Christ. But most importantly, we will see Jesus who has come to meet us in the air. When we see Him, we will be comforted with the truth that we will be with Christ forever.

The Rapture 3

IT COULD HAPPEN AT ANY MOMENT!

There is nothing left in history to stop Jesus Christ from coming for His followers today. The very thought of Christ returning for you and me at any time should give us great joy and anticipation. In the twinkling of an eye, because of Christ, our whole existence will be changed forever. God wants these thoughts to forever encourage us. The Bible says in 1 Thessalonians 4:18 —

> 1 Thessalonians 4:18 (NIV)
> *"Therefore encourage each other with these words."*

4 | The Antichrist

4 The Antichrist

The Rapture of Christians during the end times will be an incredible event. It will shake up those who will be left behind. Millions of Christians will suddenly be taken from the earth. But those left behind will have relatively little time to think about all the missing Christians. New powerful events will soon occupy their minds. A man like no other man the world has ever known will appear before them on the stage of human history. This man will be the most brilliant and persuasive leader ever. He will also be the most vicious and wicked person to have ever walked this earth. He will skyrocket to world leadership. Though his reign will last just a few years, through military power and worldwide economic control, he will bring the world to its knees. Because of him half of the world's population will die. The Bible calls this man the Antichrist.

> **IN THIS CHAPTER, WE WILL ATTEMPT TO GET A GLIMPSE OF THE MOST POWERFUL AND HORRIBLE MAN WHO WILL EVER LIVE — THE ANTICHRIST.**

4 | **The Antichrist**

I. THE BIBLE TELLS US THAT THE ANTICHRIST WILL BE A TRULY AMAZING MAN WHO WILL APPEAR ON THE WORLD STAGE DURING THE END TIMES.

The world has never seen anyone quite like the Antichrist. While there have been other powerful world leaders, none will be able to compare with the Antichrist's charisma and power. This man will be so intelligent that he will appear to have all the solutions to the world's problems. He will be such a tremendous communicator that he will hold the world spellbound. He will be such an awesome military leader that he will rule over the entire world.

The book of Daniel in the Old Testament is an amazing book. In it we find detailed visions from God to the prophet Daniel concerning the end times. Some of these visions are long and detailed. They also need careful interpretation. Yet, it is obvious that in Daniel 7:8 and 20, God is clearly speaking of the Antichrist. In these two passages, Daniel describes some of the qualities of the Antichrist:

Daniel 7:8, 20 (RSV)

8) "I considered the horns, and behold, there came up among them another horn, a little one, before which three of the first horns were plucked up by the roots; and behold, in this horn were <u>eyes like the eyes of a man</u>, and a <u>mouth speaking great things</u>.

20) and concerning the ten horns that were on its head, and the other horn which came up and before which three of them fell, the horn which had <u>eyes</u> and a <u>mouth that spoke great things</u>, and which <u>seemed greater than its fellows</u>."

---

4 | The Antichrist

The Antichrist | 4

In Daniel 7:8 and 20 Daniel spoke of the Antichrist's eyes. He said the Antichrist would have 'eyes like the eyes of a man.' What do you think that phrase means?

_____

_____

_____

A. THE ANTICHRIST WILL BE A SUPER GENIUS.

The words 'had eyes' or 'eyes' in Hebrew refer to a person's intellect, brilliance, and cleverness. The Antichrist will be the most brilliant man who has ever lived. He will have supernatural mental abilities and insights. This man will develop a master plan to solve all of the world's political and economic problems. He will be able to master facts and ideas and recite them back to the world better than any computer could ever do. The world will be in awe of this genius.

B. THE ANTICHRIST WILL BE AN AWESOME COMMUNICATOR.

In Daniel 7:8 and 20, Daniel says that the Antichrist will have a 'mouth that spoke great things.'

What do you think that phrase means?

_____

_____

_____

_____

Basically a 'mouth that spoke great things' refers to the fact that the Antichrist will be a tremendous communicator. He will master the modern forms of communication far better than any leader ever has. His worldwide audience will no doubt feel that they know him personally. He will appear charming and kind, yet cause deep emotions and passion in those who listen to him speak. So persuasive will this man be that he will be able to talk tens of millions of people into following him and doing whatever he wants them to do.

C. THE ANTICHRIST WILL BE A GREAT LEADER.

Daniel, in Daniel 7:20 said, '...*seemed greater than it's fellows.*' What do you think that means?

_____

_____

_____

_____

Daniel compares the Antichrist to other leaders of his time. In comparison, the Antichrist seemed greater. The Antichrist will be the greatest leader this world has ever known. He will have a magnetism and power that will be irresistible to the world. People will naturally want to follow him. They will look to him as their only hope. The generals of all the armies of the world will take their orders from the Antichrist. The world will breathlessly wait for his latest thought, idea or command. In fact the Bible says in Revelation 13:7b —

The Antichrist | 4

> Revelation 13:7b (NIV)
> *"And he was given authority over every tribe, people, language and nation."*

In the end times the world will be confused and chaotic. The masses of humanity will long for someone who offers them personal peace and security. The hunger, hurt and problems of the world will be so intense that people will be suckers for his deceptive line — his promise to make everything right. The Antichrist will be the one who will come and give that hope and security to the masses of people around the world. So great will the Antichrist be that John says of him in Revelation 13:3—

> Revelation 13:3b (NIV)
> *"The whole world was astonished and followed the beast."*

The Antichrist

II. THE ANTICHRIST WILL COME OUT OF THE MOST POWERFUL EMPIRE IN HISTORY. HE WILL BE EMPOWERED BY SATAN.

It will be too bad for the world when the Antichrist rules. At that time the world will soon become a very unhappy place. This leader, who is such a genius, communicator, and motivator of the masses, will turn out to be the most evil and destructive man that ever lived.

A. THE ANTICHRIST WILL COME OUT OF THE MOST POWERFUL AND GODLESS EMPIRE IN HISTORY — THE ROMAN EMPIRE.

The prophet Daniel was shown a troubling vision of the ferocious leader who will appear during the end times. This vision seen by Daniel clearly explains that the Antichrist will come out of the most powerful and godless empire in all history. In Daniel chapter 7, we read of Daniel's vision.

Daniel 7:2-8; 15-17; 19-25; 28 (NIV)
2) "Daniel said: 'In my vision at night I looked, and there before me were the four winds of heaven churning up the _great sea_.
3) Four great beasts, each different from the others, came up out of the sea.
4) The first was like a _lion_, and it had the wings of an eagle. I watched until its wings were torn off and it was lifted from the ground so that it stood on two feet like a man, and the heart of a man was given to it.
5) And there before me was a second beast, which looked like a _bear_. It was raised up on one of its sides, and it had three ribs in its mouth between its teeth. It was told, 'Get up and eat your fill of flesh!'
6) After that, I looked, and there before me was another beast, one that looked like a _leopard_. And on its back it had four wings like those of a bird. This beast had four heads, and it was given authority to rule.
7) After that, in my vision at night I looked, and there before me was a _fourth beast_ - terrifying and frightening and very powerful. It had large iron teeth; it crushed and devoured its victims and trampled underfoot whatever was left. It was different from all the former beasts, and it had ten horns.

'Great sea' — history's mass of humanity.

'Lion' — The lion represents the great Babylonian empire led by Nebuchadnezzar, king of Babylon. It was known for its strength, ferociousness, destructiveness and quickness of movement.

'Bear' — The bear represents the Medo-Persian empire led by Darius. It was known for being fierce, raging with hunger and devouring all in its path.

'Leopard' — The leopard represents the Grecian empire led by Alexander the Great. It was known for its swiftness and wide-reaching domination.

'Fourth beast' — A terrifying beast that has never been seen or understood by humans.

4 | The Antichrist

8) While I was thinking about the horns, there <u>before me was another horn, a little one, which came up among them</u>; and three of the first horns were uprooted before it. This horn had eyes like the eyes of a man and a mouth that spoke boastfully.

15) I, Daniel, was troubled in spirit, and the visions that passed through my mind disturbed me.

16) I approached one of those standing there and asked him the true meaning of all this. So he told me and gave me the interpretation of these things:

17) <u>The four great beasts are four kingdoms that will rise from the earth</u>.

19) Then I wanted to know the true meaning of the fourth beast, which was different from all the others and most terrifying, with its iron teeth and bronze claws - the beast that crushed and devoured its victims and trampled underfoot whatever was left.

20) I also wanted to know about the ten horns on its head and about the <u>other horn that came up</u>, before which three of them fell - the horn that looked more imposing than the others and that had eyes and a mouth that spoke boastfully.

21) As I watched, this horn was waging war against the saints and defeating them,

This fourth beast represents the great Roman empire. It was known for its absolute crushing and destroying of its enemies. The Roman empire was by far the most powerful, vicious, consuming empire the world has ever known.

Daniel is speaking of the Antichrist (the little horn) who will somehow be raised up out of a renewal of the old Roman empire.

Daniel was particularly concerned about this 'other horn' on this beast. 'Horn' speaks of strength and honor; it is a means of attack and defense, therefore an emblem of power, authority, and rule.

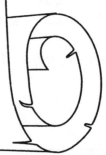

22) until the <u>Ancient of Days</u> came and pronounced judgment in favor of the saints of the Most High, and the time came when they possessed the kingdom. 23) He gave me this explanation: <u>The fourth beast is a fourth kingdom that will appear on earth. It will be different from all other kingdoms and will devour the whole earth, trampling it down and crushing it.</u> 24) <u>The ten horns are ten kings who will come from this kingdom.</u> After them <u>another king will arise</u>, different from the earlier ones; he will subdue three kings. 25) He will speak against the Most High and oppress his saints and try to change the set times and the laws. <u>The saints will be handed over to him for a time, times and half a time.</u> 28) This is the end of the matter. I, Daniel, was deeply troubled by my thoughts, and my face turned pale, but I kept the matter to myself."

The *'Ancient of Days'* is none other than the Messiah - Jesus Christ who will come and destroy the Antichrist.

This fourth kingdom is the Roman empire.

Daniel predicted that there would be a ten nation confederacy that would arise out of the old Roman empire.

'Another king will arise' refers to the Antichrist who will suppress three kings from the renewal of the old Roman empire.

'Time, times, and half a time' refers to three and a half years of intense suffering.

4 | The Antichrist

The Antichrist $\boxed{4}$

As we can see from the vision of Daniel, this Antichrist will arise out of the old Roman Empire. The other world leaders such as Nebuchadnezzar, Darius, Alexander the Great, and the Roman Caesars pale in comparison to this remarkable but vile man. The Antichrist will be more powerful than any other world leader in history.

B.   SATAN WILL POSSESS THE ANTICHRIST.

Who will make the Antichrist so incredibly ruthless? Who will make him the very picture of evil? From whom does he get his world-conquering power? In the book of Revelation, the Apostle John was also given visions of the end times. In Revelation 13:2, he tells us who is the source of the Antichrist:

Revelation 13:2 (NIV)
"The beast I saw resembled a leopard, but had feet like those of a bear and a mouth like that of a lion. The dragon gave the beast his power and his throne and great authority."

According to Revelation 13:2, what gives the Antichrist his power and is the very source of his wickedness?

_____

_____

_____

_____

The Antichrist

We know from Revelation 12:9 that the 'dragon' is none other than Satan himself. Satan will possess the Antichrist and give him power and authority which the world has never seen. Satan will possess the Antichrist and use him to carry out his Satanic plan.

Is it any wonder that the Antichrist will be full of power and do miraculous things before the eyes of an unsuspecting world? The Apostle Paul talked about this in 2 Thessalonians 2:9-10 —

2 Thessalonians 2:9-10 (NIV)
9) "The coming of the lawless one will be in accordance with the work of Satan displayed in all kinds of counterfeit miracles, signs and wonders,
10) and in every sort of evil that deceives those who are perishing...."

4 | The Antichrist

III. THE ANTICHRIST, EMPOWERED BY THE DRAGON, WILL WORK VICIOUSLY TO CARRY OUT SATAN'S PLAN.

A. SATAN'S PLAN HAS ALWAYS BEEN TO BE AGAINST CHRIST, AND TO PUT HIMSELF AS THE CENTER OF ALL WORSHIP.

There is nothing new about Satan's plan. Since his rebellion towards God in heaven, he has always been against the Lord. Satan has always hated God the Son — Jesus Christ. Christ defeated Satan at the Cross. Notice what Luke and Paul write concerning Christ's power over Satan:

> Luke 10:17-18 (NIV)
> *17) "The seventy-two returned with joy and said, 'Lord, even the demons submit to us in your name.'*
> *18) He replied, 'I saw Satan fall like lightning from heaven.'"*
>
> Colossians 2:15 (NIV)
> *"And having disarmed the powers and authorities, he made a public spectacle of them, triumphing over them by the cross."*

Satan down to the very last moment of time will viciously fight against Jesus. In the end times, Satan will reveal his newest weapon — the Antichrist. The Bible talks about this in 1 John 2:18 —

The Antichrist | 4

> 1 John 2:18 (NIV)
> *"Dear children, this is the last hour; and as you have heard that the antichrist is coming, even now many antichrists have come. This is how we know it is the last hour."*

What do you think 'antichrist' means?

_____

_____

_____

'Anti' means to 'stand up against.' Satan has always worked through those who refuse to come to God, who stand up against God and His truth. But as Satan sees his time running out, he will increase his opposition to God. The intensity of Satan's hatred for God will show itself in the rage, arrogance, and evil of the Antichrist. It will be through the Antichrist that Satan will reveal his most heartfelt desire. That desire is to be worshipped as God. The Bible talks about this in 2 Thessalonians 2:3-4 —

> 2 Thessalonians 2:3-4 (NIV)
> *3) "Don't let anyone deceive you in any way, for that day will not come until the rebellion occurs and the man of lawlessness is revealed, the man doomed to destruction.*
> *4) He will oppose and exalt himself over everything that is called God or is worshipped, so that he sets himself up in God's temple, proclaiming himself to be God."*

B. SATAN'S PLAN THROUGH THE ANTICHRIST WILL BE TO DESTROY THOSE WHO BELIEVE IN CHRIST.

Satan not only violently hates Christ but also those who believe in Christ. Down through the ages, true believers have been severely persecuted by Satan through a world that does not know Christ. Yet at the end of time, Satan will work through the Antichrist to seek to wipe out everyone on this earth who believes in Jesus. This persecution of true believers through the Antichrist will be the greatest attack in the history of mankind. The Bible talks about this vicious attack in Revelation 13:7-8 —

Revelation 13:7-8 (NAS)
7) *"And it was given to him to make war with the saints and to overcome them; and authority over every tribe and people and tongue and nation was given to him.*
8) *And all who dwell on the earth will worship him, every one whose name has not been written from the foundation of the world in the book of life of the Lamb who has been slain."*

According to Revelation 13:7, what does Satan want to do to Christians through the Antichrist?

_____

_____

_____

_____

According to Revelation 13:8, how successful will the Antichrist be in getting others to worship him?

_____

_____

_____

     In conclusion, many people have asked this simple question: Is the Antichrist alive today? No one knows for certain. But this much we do know — he is coming. He will come on the world stage acting as a 'savior.' But tragically in the end, since he is controlled by Satan, he will be the great destroyer! As we shall see, the Antichrist will be destroyed by Christ Himself. It will be a terrifying time to live during the reign of the Antichrist. Yet, those of us who believe in Christ can find comfort in God's love, power and protection even in the worst of times. The Bible speaks of both the awfulness of this world at the end when Satan shows his fury and the joy of knowing Christ in Revelation 12:12 —

Revelation 12:12 (TLB)
"Rejoice, O heavens! You citizens of heaven, rejoice! Be glad! But woe to you people of the world, for the devil has come down to you in great anger, knowing that he has little time."

5 The Great Tribulation — Part One

As we saw in the last chapter, events in the end times will happen rapidly. Once the Antichrist appears on the scene, things will occur at an incredible pace. What will happen at the end will lead to a horrible tragedy. The Bible tells us that a time is coming that will be more traumatic and terrifying than any thing you and I could imagine. The Bible calls this seven year period the Great Tribulation.

What is the Tribulation?

The Tribulation is a seven year period that takes place before the Second Coming of Jesus Christ. It will be a time when Satan reigns through the Antichrist, when men show their absolute rebellion towards God, and God pours out His judgments on mankind.

Jesus spoke of just how awful the Tribulation period would be when He said in Matthew 24:21-22 —

Matthew 24:21-22 (NIV)
21) *"For then there will be great distress, unequaled from the beginning of the world until now - and never to be equaled again.*
22) *If those days had not been cut short, no one would survive, but for the sake of the elect those days will be shortened."*

5 | The Great Tribulation — Part One

Tim LaHaye, in his book 'No Fear of the Storm,' writes,

"Jesus predicted that, due to its appalling nature, the Tribulation will be shortened. It will become such a holocaust because it combines the wrath of God, the fury of Satan, and the evil nature of man run wild. Take the horror of every war since time began, throw in every natural disaster in recorded history, and cast off all restraints so that the unspeakable cruelty and hatred and injustice of man toward his fellow men can fully mature…then compress it all into a period of seven years. Even if you could imagine such a thing, it wouldn't approach the mind-boggling terror and turmoil of the Tribulation."[1]

> **IN THIS STUDY, WE WILL TRY TO GRASP THE INCREDIBLE EVENTS THAT WILL TAKE PLACE IN THE FIRST HALF OF THE TRIBULATION.**

[1] Tim LaHaye, *No Fear Of The Storm* (Sisters, Oregon: Questar Publishers, Inc., 1992), 50

The Great Tribulation — Part One   5

I. THE ANTICHRIST WILL USE DIPLOMACY AND DECEPTION TO GAIN POWER.

As we saw in the last chapter, the Antichrist will arise out of the old Roman Empire. In Daniel's prophecy, he saw a coming ten nation confederacy that would arise out of what is now known as Europe. The Antichrist will use his political brilliance to take over this ten nation confederacy. Daniel speaks about this in Daniel 7:7-8 —

Daniel 7:7-8 (NIV)
7) "After that, in my vision at night I looked, and there before me was a <u>fourth beast</u> - terrifying and frightening and very powerful. It had large iron teeth; it crushed and devoured its victims and trampled underfoot whatever was left. It was different from all the former beasts, and it had <u>ten horns</u>.
8) While I was thinking about the horns, there before me was <u>another horn, a little one, which came up among them</u>; and <u>three of the first horns</u> were uprooted before it. This horn had eyes like the eyes of a man and a mouth that spoke boastfully."

Further on in Daniel 7, the prophet was given the interpretation or explanation of what he saw in Daniel 7:23-24 —

Daniel 7:23-24 (NIV)
23) "He gave me this explanation: 'The <u>fourth beast is a fourth kingdom</u> that will appear on earth. It will be different from all other kingdoms and will devour the whole earth, trampling it down and crushing it.
24) The <u>ten horns are ten kings</u> who will come from this kingdom. After them another king will arise, different from the earlier ones; he will subdue three kings."

A. THE ANTICHRIST WILL RISE TO POWER THROUGH A TEN NATION CONFEDERACY.

In these two passages, we (the authors) have underlined some key words. These will help us understand more clearly Daniel's prophecy.

Understanding These Important Words

(1) What is the 'fourth beast'? — The fourth beast represents the old Roman Empire. Until the coming of the Antichrist, it was the most frightening world empire to exist.

(2) What are the 'ten horns'? — The ten horns represent ten rulers or kings who will make up a European ten nation confederacy.

(3) What is 'another horn, a little one, which came up among them'? — This little horn is none other than the Antichrist who arises from within the ten nation confederacy.

(4) What are 'the three horns'? — The three horns are three kings who come to power in the ten nation confederacy. These three kings will lose their power to the Antichrist. (See Revelation 17:12-13; and Daniel 11:21-24).

The Bible tells us that this diplomatic genius will be so smooth and clever that he will take over the entire ten kingdoms (nations) with relative ease. Early on in the Tribulation, this master politician will begin to seize tremendous power.

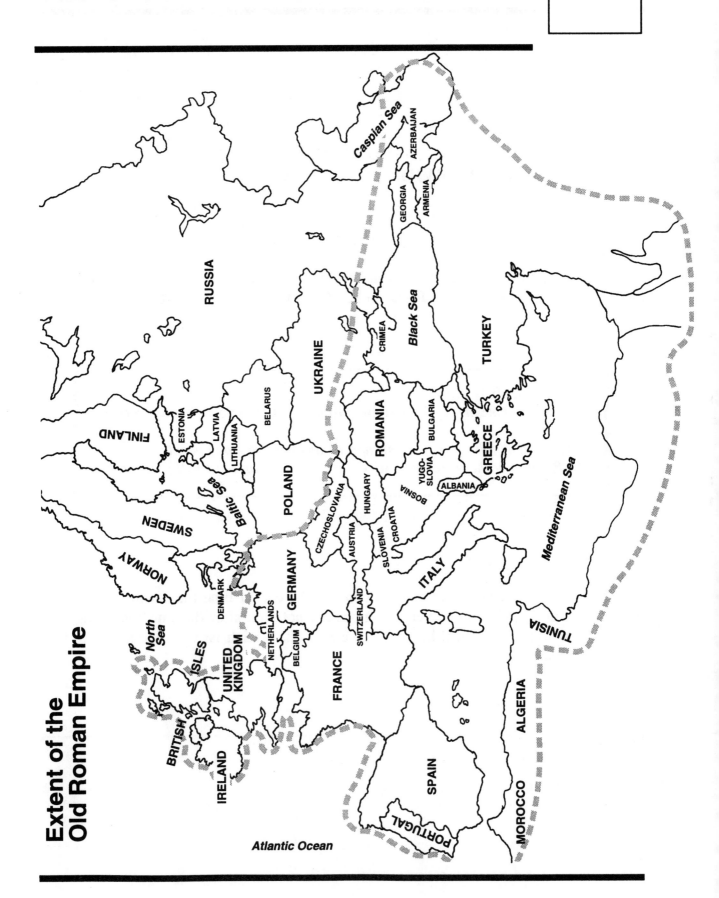

Extent of the
Old Roman Empire

B. THE ANTICHRIST WILL FORM AN UNHOLY ALLIANCE WITH A WORLDWIDE RELIGION.

By the time the Antichrist appears on the world stage, the masses will have turned away from God's truth. Jesus spoke of this turning away in Matthew 24:10-12:

Matthew 24:10-12 (NIV)
10) "At that time many will turn away from the faith and will betray and hate each other,
11) and many false prophets will appear and deceive many people.
12) Because of the increase of wickedness, the love of most will grow cold."

The Bible clearly teaches us that as we come to the end of time there will be a one-world religion. People will be very religious but not seek after the true and living God. This world religion will be very powerful. The Antichrist will find a way to link up with this false faith.

The Great Tribulation — Part One | 5

The Apostle John in a vision from God was shown the unholy alliance that will take place between the Antichrist and Worldwide Religion in Revelation 17:3-6 —

Revelation 17:3-6 (NIV)
3) "Then the angel carried me away in the Spirit into a desert. There I saw a <u>woman</u> sitting on a scarlet <u>beast</u> that was covered with blasphemous names and had seven heads and ten horns.
4) The woman was dressed in purple and scarlet, and was glittering with gold, precious stones and pearls. She held a golden cup in her hand, filled with abominable things and the filth of her adulteries.
5) This title was written on her forehead:

MYSTERY
BABYLON THE GREAT
THE MOTHER OF PROSTITUTES
AND OF THE ABOMINATIONS OF
THE EARTH.

6) I saw that the woman was drunk with the blood of the <u>saints</u>, the blood of those who bore testimony to Jesus."

In Revelation 17:3-6, we find phrases and imagery that make it difficult to understand. Yet when we consider the characters being discussed it is easier for us to comprehend its meaning.

The Great Tribulation — Part One | 5

The Three Characters of Revelation 17

In Revelation 17:3-6, we are told that John in his vision saw three characters.

(1) The Prostitute Woman

In the vision that John saw there appeared a woman that was no ordinary woman.

Why do you think this woman in John's vision was no ordinary woman?

_____

_____

_____

_____

_____

It is clear from Revelation 17:3-6, that God is disgusted with this 'woman.' She is dressed beautifully and expensively. But she has in her hand a golden cup that is "filled with abominable things and the filth of her adulteries." In the Bible, the term adultery is often used in a spiritual way. Notice what these verses are saying:

Jeremiah 3:9 (NIV)
"Because Israel's immorality mattered so little to her, she defiled the land and committed adultery with stone and wood."

> Hosea 4:12 (NIV)
> *"They consult a wooden idol and are answered by a stick of wood. A spirit of prostitution leads them astray; they are unfaithful to their God."*

Adultery in the Bible can represent man's unfaithfulness to God. This 'woman' represents people who have turned away from God, who are living in a spiritually adulterous way and are no longer faithful to Him.

In Revelation 17:5 a title was given to this woman:

"MYSTERY — BABYLON THE GREAT — THE MOTHER OF PROSTITUTES AND OF THE ABOMINATIONS OF THE EARTH."

What do you think the title on this woman's forehead means?

_____

_____

_____

_____

_____

This woman is called Babylon. In the Bible, the city of Babylon represents man turning away from God and seeking spiritual answers through his own efforts and astrology. This woman represents a world religion that has turned away from God and seeks to make up its own religion apart from him.

(2) The Beast.

The Apostle John in his vision saw a woman who was sitting on a scarlet beast. This beast is none other than the Antichrist. He is covered with wicked names that prove his rebellion towards God.

(3) The Saints.

John also saw that the people who believe in Jesus Christ would be persecuted by this false religion. This counterfeit faith will seek to combine a little of everyone's religion. Yet, it will hate and seek to kill anyone who worships the true and living God.

Unholy Alliance

Early in the Tribulation period two powerful forces will meet. The Antichrist, who will be the head of a ten nation confederacy will unite with Worldwide Religion. No doubt both of these powerful forces will see that they should join together and become stronger than ever. It will look like a stroke of genius for these two powers to become partners. But only one party will end up being the winner in this power dance of death.

C. THE ANTICHRIST WILL FORM AN ALLIANCE WITH ISRAEL

In the early days of the Tribulation, the Antichrist will be very busy. Using his political skills and his ability to deceive, he will be making alliances and adding more power to himself. He will work his way into control of the ten nation confederacy. He will also make an incredible pact with the forces of world religion. But perhaps his greatest move will be his alliance with the nation of Israel.

As we know, Israel is one of the most strategic, yet hated, nations in the world. God's people, the Jews, reside there. And as we head into the end times it will be a focal point of history. Current news tells us that there has never been a solution for peace in the Middle East. Try as they may, world leaders cannot find the formula for lasting peace in that volatile region of the world.

Why do you think peace in the Middle East has been all but impossible to find?

_____

_____

_____

_____

_____

The Great Tribulation — Part One | 5

When the Antichrist appears, he will develop a peace plan that will seemingly solve the riddle of hate in the Middle East. It may very well be the greatest stroke of political genius ever played out on the world stage. Part of that plan for peace for Israel will be an alliance between Israel and the Antichrist. The prophet Daniel foretold of the deceitful yet powerful moves of the Antichrist to seduce Israel into putting her trust in him. This is found in Daniel 9 and 11 —

> Daniel 9:27 (TLB)
> *"This king will make a seven-year treaty with the people, but after half that time, he will break his pledge and stop the Jews from all their sacrifices and their offerings; then, as a climax to all his terrible deeds, the Enemy shall utterly defile the sanctuary of God. But in God's time and plan, his judgment will be poured out upon this Evil One."*

> Daniel 11:21-23 (TLB)
> *21) "Next to come to power will be an evil man not directly in line for royal succession. But during a crisis he will take over the kingdom by flattery and intrigue.*
> *22) Then all opposition will be swept away before him, including a leader of the priests.*
> *23) His promises will be worthless. From the first his method will be deceit; with a mere handful of followers, he will become strong."*

The Antichrist will be truly amazing. He will be able to lull Israel into trusting him for their protection. This evil man will be so smug and confident that he will be able to control the events that will take place in the Middle East. He no doubt will reason that if he can control Israel and the Middle East, he will be able to control the world. But suddenly with little warning, events will seem to destroy his well-thought-out plans for world dominance.

II. THE GREAT ARMIES OF THE RUSSIAN ALLIANCE WILL ATTACK ISRAEL.

The Antichrist will amass a lot of power in the early months and years of the Tribulation. Yet, there will be some nations who will not yet have fallen under his sway. One of the great nations that will remain independent of the Antichrist will be Russia. Russia and her allies will have plans of their own to take over Israel.

The Bible tells us that in the end times Russia will have a plan to invade and plunder Israel. She and her allies will want to take the rich minerals and wealth that Israel will have accumulated. The problem for Russia and her friends will be that they will fail to understand who they are fighting. Instead of simply fighting the Israelis, they will do battle with God Himself. Russia and her allies will all but be destroyed in this Great War. In Ezekiel 38 and 39, we are told the moving events of what will happen when this great army from the North does battle with Israel. Let us look at Ezekiel 38 and 39 to learn about this Great War.

The Great Tribulation — Part One | 5

A. WHO ARE THE PLAYERS IN THIS GREAT WAR?

The prophet Ezekiel predicted the major countries who would attack Israel. He spoke of those countries in Ezekiel 38:1-7 —

Ezekiel 38:1-7 (TLB)
1) *"Here is another message to me from the Lord:*
2) *'Son of dust, face northward toward the land of Magog and prophesy against Gog king of Meshech and Tubal.*
3) *Tell him that the Lord God says: 'I am against you, Gog.*
4) *I will put hooks into your jaws and pull you to your doom. I will mobilize your troops and armored cavalry, and make you a mighty host, all fully armed.*
5) *Peras, Cush, and Put shall join you too with all their weaponry,*
6) *and so shall Gomer and all his hordes and the armies of Togarmah from the distant north, as well as many others.*
7) *Be prepared! Stay mobilized. You are their leader, Gog!'"*

It is important that we try to identify the names that were given to Ezekiel in Ezekiel 38. By identifying these names we will be able to understand what countries will attempt to destroy Israel during the Tribulation.

1) What Role did Ezekiel predict for Russia in the Great War?

Ezekiel predicted that Russia would be involved in the great war. We find in Ezekiel 38:2-3 ancient names of those who will attack Israel in the end times:

> Ezekiel 38:2-3a (TLB)
> *"Son of dust, face northward toward the land of <u>Magog</u> and prophesy against <u>Gog</u> king of <u>Meshech</u> and <u>Tubal</u>."*

Magog
The name Magog is first found in Genesis 10. He was the grandson of Noah and a son of Japtheth. Magog in time moved northward beyond the Black sea and the famous Caucaus mountains. This region is now known as Russia.

Gog
Most Bible scholars agree that Gog is the king of Russia. As we have studied Russia over the centuries, we know that her government has not been a democracy but a kingdom or dictatorship. In the end times, Russia will no doubt be led by a strong militaristic leader.

Meshech
Meshech was the ancient name of the now famous city Moscow. It represents a province or region of Russia.

Tubal
The name Tubal can be traced to the city of Tobolsk, an ancient capital in Siberia. Like Meshech, Tubal represents a province or region of Russia.

The prophet Ezekiel is very clear. The region north of Israel that will wage war against her in the end times will be that menacing military might — Russia herself.

2) Who are the Russian Allies?

Not only does Ezekiel pinpoint Russia as Israel's enemy but also identifies Russia's allies who will also fight against Israel.

> Ezekiel 38:5-6 (TLB)
> 5) *"Peras, Cush, and Put shall join you too with all their weaponry,*
> 6) *and so shall Gomer and all his hordes and the armies of Togarmah from the distant north, as well as many others."*

Peras
The modern name Persia can be traced to the ancient name Peras. Persia includes such modern nations as Iran, Iraq, and most of the Arab States.

Cush
The name Cush can be traced to the peoples of Eastern Africa. They include such countries as the Sudan and Ethopia.

Put
Put is identified by most scholars as the modern nation of Libya.

Gomer
Gomer was the oldest son of Japtheth, Noah's son. Gomer settled with his people north of the Black Sea and then moved south and west into what is now Eastern Europe. Therefore Gomer's descendants are today's Eastern Europeans.

Togarmah
Bible scholars trace the descendants of Togarmah, who in Scripture is one of the three sons of Gomer, to what is now the general vicinity of Armenia and Turkey.

The prophet Ezekiel in the first seven verses of chapter 38, tells us that Russia and her allies will pose an overwhelming threat as they march on Israel.

Russia & Her Allies

TUBAL
Tobolsk

MESCHECH
Moscow

GOMER
Ukraine

MAGOG
Germanic

TOGARMAH
Armenia

PERAS
Iran

Iraq

ISRAEL

PUT
Libya

Sudan

CUSH
Ethiopia

The Great Tribulation — Part One | 5

B.   WHAT IS RUSSIA'S VICIOUS MILITARY PLAN?

The prophet Ezekiel in Ezekiel 38:7-12 and 15-16 made some amazing predictions about the end times. Ezekiel not only predicted that Russia would attack Israel but even spelled out their motivation and plan to do it.

Ezekiel 38:7-12; 15-16a (TLB)

7) *"Be prepared! Stay mobilized. You are their leader, Gog!*

8) *A long time from now you will be called to action. In distant years you will swoop down onto the land of Israel that will be lying in peace after the return of its people from many lands.*

9) *You and all your allies - a vast and awesome army - will roll down upon them like a storm and cover the land like a cloud.*

10) *For at that time an evil thought will have come to your mind.*

11) *You will have said, 'Israel is an unprotected land of unwalled villages! I will march against her and destroy these people living in such confidence!*

12) *I will go to those once desolate cities that are now filled with people again - those who have returned from all the nations - and I will capture vast amounts of loot and many slaves. For the people are rich with cattle now, and the whole earth revolves around them!'*

15) *You will come from all over the north with your vast host of cavalry*

16) *and cover the land like a cloud. This will happen in the distant future - in the latter years of history."*

According to verse 8, Russia and her allies 'will swoop down onto the land of Israel.' What do you think that means?

_____

_____

_____

Russia and its allies will shock the rest of the world with their quick, massive, organized and brilliant invasion of Israel.

According to verse 8, Israel 'will be lying in peace.' Why do you think the ever-cautious Israeli nation will be so relaxed when the invasion takes place?

_____

_____

_____

According to verse 9 what kind of chance will the people of Israel have against this army?

_____

_____

_____

Israel will be no match for this massive military force. This army moving with lightning swift speed and tens of thousands of soldiers will simply roll over little Israel.

According to Ezekiel 38:15, Russia will come with a 'vast host of cavalry.' Why is this important?

_____

_____

_____

It's hard to believe that Russia will still be using horses in this modern war. Yet as late as World War II, Russia's cavalry met and defeated some of the more modern German forces. The invading army will have to travel through some very tough terrain. Horses are still the quickest and safest means of transporting troops, light artillery and field equipment over mountainous terrain. As we know, the land between Russia and Israel is extremely mountainous.

In Ezekiel 38:10-12, the prophet shares with us the reasons why Russia and her allies will invade Israel. According to those two verses why do you think Russia will want to invade Israel?

_____

_____

_____

The Great Tribulation — Part One | 5

The Bible tells us that there are many reasons why Russia will want to invade Israel. First, through the centuries, Israel has been hated by their neighbors. Perhaps Russia and her allies will see a chance to wipe out Israel once and for all. Secondly, Russia will see that Israel is unprotected and living in confidence. Evidently Russia and her allies will understand that the Antichrist will not come to Israel's rescue. Thirdly, Russia will clearly understand the vast amount of riches that Israel will offer. They will have not only such riches as gold, minerals, and cattle, but Israel will also have people who can be used as slaves once they are conquered. Finally, the Middle East has always been the center of world activity. Russia and her allies will want all the religious and political power that comes with control of that part of the world. The alliance's greed for power, plunder, and hatred will cause them to move to destroy Israel.

C.   HOW WILL GOD STEP IN AND FIGHT FOR ISRAEL?

As Russia and her allies cover Israel it will look as though Israel will have no hope. The countries that are allied to the West and the Western powers themselves (the Antichrist and his nations) will be very bothered about the invasion. Ezekiel talks about the enemies of Russia and their alliance. In Ezekiel 38:13, the Bible tells us of their complaint:

> Ezekiel 38:13 (TLB)
> *"But Sheba and Dedan and the merchant princes of Tarshish with whom she trades will ask, 'Who are you to rob them of silver and gold and drive away their cattle and seize their goods and make them poor?'"*

But their complaint to the Russia Alliance will fall on deaf ears. The brutal Russian forces and their friends will be determined to crush Israel. It will appear that all is lost for Israel.

The Great Tribulation — Part One

5

God Pours Out His Wrath on the Russian Alliance.

The Russian Alliance will come up against a force they did not plan to meet. This force will be far greater than anything they could have ever imagined. This great army from the north will encounter God Himself, who in His terrible wrath is determined to protect Israel. In Ezekiel 38:17-23, we have the account of this one-sided war with Russia, and her allies, and God Himself.

Ezekiel 38:17-23 (TLB)

17) "The Lord God says: 'You are the one I spoke of long ago through the prophets of Israel, saying that after many years had passed, I would bring you against my people.

18) But when you come to destroy the land of Israel, my fury will rise!

19) For in my jealousy and blazing wrath, I promise a mighty shaking in the land of Israel on that day.

20) All living things shall quake in terror at my presence; mountains shall be thrown down; cliffs shall tumble; walls shall crumble to the earth.

21) I will summon every kind of terror against you,' says the Lord God, 'and you will fight against yourselves in mortal combat!

22) I will fight you with sword, disease, torrential floods, great hailstones, fire and brimstone!

23) Thus will I show my greatness and bring honor upon my name, and all the nations of the world will hear what I have done, and know that I am God!'"

According to Ezekiel 38:18-19, how will God feel about Russia's attack on Israel?

_____

_____

_____

_____

111

5 | The Great Tribulation — Part One

According to Ezekiel 38:20, what is one of the means God will use to defeat the Russian army?

_____

_____

_____

_____

According to Ezekiel 38:21-22, what are some other means God will use to destroy His enemy?

_____

_____

_____

_____

According to Ezekiel 38:23, what will be the response of every nation in the world to this war between God and the Russian Alliance?

_____

_____

_____

The Great Tribulation — Part One | 5

The Russian Alliance Pays a Terrible Price for Waging War Against Israel.

In Ezekiel 39 verses 1 through 12, God explains the horrible price Russia will pay for her attack on Israel:

Ezekiel 39:1-12 (TLB)

1) "Son of dust, prophesy this also against Gog. Tell him: 'I will stand against you, Gog, leader of Meshech and Tubal.

2) I will turn you and drive you toward the mountains of Israel, bringing you from the distant north. And I will destroy 85 percent of your army in the mountains.

3) I will knock your weapons from your hands and leave you helpless.

4) You and all your vast armies will die upon the mountains. I will give you to the vultures and wild animals to devour you.

5) You will never reach the cities - you will fall upon the open fields; for I have spoken, the Lord God says.

6) And I will rain down fire on Magog and on all your allies who live safely on the coasts, and they shall know I am the Lord.

7) Thus I will make known my holy name among my people Israel; I will not let it be mocked at anymore. And the nations, too, shall know I am the Lord, the Holy One of Israel.

8) That day of judgment will come; everything will happen just as I have declared it.

9) The people of the cities of Israel will go out and pick up your shields and bucklers, bows and arrows, javelins and spears, to use for fuel - enough to last them seven years.

10) For seven years they will need nothing else for their fires. They won't cut wood from the fields or forests, for these weapons will give them all they need. They will use the possessions of those who abused them.

11) And I will make a vast graveyard for Gog and his armies in the Valley of the Travelers, east of the Dead Sea. It will block the path of the travelers. There Gog and all his armies will be buried. And they will change the name of the place to 'The Valley of Gog's Army.'

12) It will take seven months for the people of Israel to bury the bodies."

5 | The Great Tribulation — Part One

PROJECT - The Terrible Consequences for the Russian Alliance

Read through Ezekiel 39:1-12 and list the terrible things that will happen to the Russian Alliance.

_____

_____

_____

_____

_____

_____

_____

_____

What a terrible price the Russian Alliance will pay for their attack on Israel! The whole world will clearly understand that it was God who defeated the mighty army of the Russian Alliance.

People living at the time of this mighty war will be amazed at God's power. They will know that it is He who defeated the Russian army. Yet, they will continue to turn away from God and go on their rebellious ways. Little will they understand that they will be marching to their final doom.

III. IN THE TRIBULATION, GOD HIMSELF WILL RAISE UP MIGHTY SPOKESMEN TO PREACH CHRIST TO A TOTALLY REBELLIOUS WORLD.

The Antichrist no doubt will first be terrified when he sees the invasion of Israel by Russia and her allies. Whatever the Antichrist will try to do to stop this great invasion will not work. But what will start out as a bad event for the Antichrist will end up in his favor. Russia and her allies will have been destroyed and now the Antichrist can gain even more power and dominance without being hindered by the Russian Alliance. By this time the world will be in tremendous need with famines, death, inflation, natural disasters and all kinds of hardships. The Antichrist will step into this vacuum with his plan to rule the world and to be worshipped.

The Antichrist will still have to deal with God. Even though the world is quickly turning into a place of total rebellion and death, God will move through the world to proclaim Christ. During the tribulation, God will raise up some of the most powerful missionaries for Christ the world has ever seen.

The Great Tribulation — Part One   5

A.   GOD'S TWO WITNESSES

In Revelation 11, the Apostle John tells us of two powerful spokesmen for God. These men will appear like Old Testament prophets powerfully preaching the Gospel and God's judgment to a world in rebellion. John said of these two men in Revelation 11:3 —

Revelation 11:3 (NIV)
"And I will give power to my two witnesses, and they will prophesy for 1,260 days, clothed in sackcloth."

According to Revelation 11:3, how long will these two witnesses prophesy for God?

_____

_____

_____

_____

Who do you think these two prophets are?

_____

_____

_____

_____

No one is totally certain as to the identity of these two incredible men. Some scholars believe that the Bible points to two men from the Old Testament. One of these Old Testament prophets is Elijah. In Malachi 3:1-3, there is a prediction that Elijah would come and prepare the way for the Messiah. It is also true that these two witnesses had much the same powers as Elijah had in that he was able to stop the rain. (James 5:17-18).

The other great witness may well be the Old Testament prophet Moses. Moses did appear during Christ's time on earth. (Matthew 17:1-9; Mark 9:2-13; Luke 9:28-36). He also showed powers in the Old Testament much like the power of God's two witnesses (Exodus 7:19-20). While no one knows for sure, Moses and Elijah may very well be not only great men of the Old Testament but also mighty spokesmen for God in the end times.

God's Two Witnesses will have Tremendous Power

John went on to explain the incredible power that God's two witnesses will have. He said in Revelation 11:5-6 —

> Revelation 11:5-6 (NIV)
> 5) *"If anyone tries to harm them, fire comes from their mouths and devours their enemies. This is how anyone who wants to harm them must die.*
> 6) *These men have power to shut up the sky so that it will not rain during the time they are prophesying; and they have power to turn the waters into blood and to strike the earth with every kind of plague as often as they want."*

The Great Tribulation — Part One

These men will be hated by most of the people who hear them. Many people will want to kill them but will be unable to.

According to Revelation 11:5, what will happen to anyone who tries to harm the two witnesses?

_____

_____

_____

_____

These two incredible witnesses will proclaim a message of judgment and will back up what they say by calling down judgment even as they speak.

According to Revelation 11:6, what kind of judgment do these two witnesses use to prove that what they are saying is true and have the power of God to back them up?

_____

_____

_____

_____

The world will be terrified and furious at these two witnesses of God. People living in the world at that time will want to forget the true and living God. Because of the two witnesses the masses will be reminded that there is a God who will act in judgment. Most of the world will absolutely hate these two witnesses and long for the day when they will die.

The Great Tribulation — Part One | 5

B.   GOD'S 144,000 JEWISH COMMANDOS FOR CHRIST

God's two powerful witnesses are not the only ones who will be preaching Christ during the Tribulation. John tells us that there will be 144,000 mighty Jewish evangelists out telling everyone about Jesus. These Jewish evangelists may have been greatly influenced by God's two witnesses. These 144,000 Jews may well be the greatest witnesses for Christ this world has ever seen. John explains who these witnesses are and what their work will be in Revelation 7:1-9 —

Revelation 7:1-9 (TLB)

1) *"Then I saw four angels standing at the four corners of the earth, holding back the four winds from blowing so that not a leaf rustled in the trees, and the ocean became as smooth as glass.*

2) *And I saw another angel coming from the east, carrying the Great Seal of the Living God. And he shouted out to those four angels who had been given power to injure earth and sea,*

3) *'Wait! Don't do anything yet - hurt neither earth nor sea nor trees - until we have placed the Seal of God upon the foreheads of his servants.'*

4-8) *How many were given this mark? I heard the number - it was 144,000; out of all twelve tribes of Israel, as listed here:*

Judah	*12,000*	*Naphtali*	*12,000*	*Issachar*	*12,000*
Reuben	*12,000*	*Manasseh*	*12,000*	*Zebulun*	*12,000*
Gad	*12,000*	*Simeon*	*12,000*	*Joseph*	*12,000*
Asher	*12,000*	*Levi*	*12,000*	*Benjamin*	*12,000*

9) *After this I saw a vast crowd, too great to count, from all nations and provinces and languages, standing in front of the throne and before the Lamb, clothed in white, with palm branches in their hands."*

According to Revelation 7:4, how do we know that these 144,000 are Jewish?

_____

_____

_____

_____

According to John's vision in Revelation 7:9, how successful do you think these evangelists will be?

_____

_____

_____

_____

The first three and one-half years of the Tribulation will be an amazing time. It will see the Antichrist rising to power. It will witness an incredible war as God destroys Russia and her allies. It will also see God raising up great spokesmen and evangelists for Christ. Yet, in spite of all of these incredible activities, it will only be the beginning of the end of the world as we know it. By the time the first half of the Tribulation is completed, the countdown to the Second Coming of Christ will be well underway. Christ will come but first the Antichrist must rule the entire world and see the awesome judgment of a holy God.

The Great Tribulation — Part One

NOTES

6 | The Great Tribulation — Part Two

T he first half of the Tribulation will be full of incredible events. God, through the Bible, tells us that all of these events will lead to the world quickly rushing to it's doom. As we enter the second half of the Tribulation we will see even more death, destruction, and judgment falling upon mankind. We will witness just how awful this world will become when the Antichrist, controlled by Satan, rules the world.

IN THIS STUDY WE WILL DISCOVER THE HORRIBLE EVENTS THAT WILL TAKE PLACE IN THE SECOND HALF OF THE GREAT TRIBULATION.

The Great Tribulation - Part Two | 6

I. EMPOWERED BY SATAN, THE ANTICHRIST WILL WORK VICIOUSLY TO TAKE OVER THE WORLD.

A. THE ANTICHRIST WILL ASTONISH THE WORLD BY BEING RESURRECTED FROM A FATAL HEAD WOUND.

The Antichrist will truly be an amazing person. He will be brilliant, a master speaker and one who will appear to have the answers to a desperate and crumbling world. By the middle of the Tribulation, he will have gained tremendous power. Yet there will be an event that will cause the world to be absolutely astounded at this man. Somehow the Antichrist will suffer a wound to his head that will lead to his death. The Apostle John saw a vision about this event and wrote about it in Revelation 13:3:

Revelation 13:3 (NIV)
"One of the heads of the beast seemed to have had a fatal wound, but the fatal wound had been healed. The whole world was astonished and followed the beast."

According to Revelation 13:3, what two things will happen to the Antichrist?

_____

_____

_____

_____

6 | The Great Tribulation - Part Two

When the world finds out that the Antichrist is dead, there will certainly be shock, sadness, and fear. The hope of the world through the Antichrist will have died. Then something truly amazing will happen. While the world mourns his death, he will come back to life. This miracle will absolutely overwhelm most people. The Bible says that the 'whole world will be astonished' by this miracle and will follow the Antichrist. The Bible tells us what these poor deceived followers of the Antichrist will be thinking:

Revelation 13:4 (NIV)
"Men worshiped the dragon because he had given authority to the beast, and they also worshiped the beast and asked, 'Who is like the beast? Who can make war against him?'"

The Antichrist will now sense a kind of power that he has never had before. He will swiftly set out to crush any opposition that stands in his way of being worshipped as God.

B. THE ANTICHRIST, IN HIS INTENSE DESIRE TO BE WORSHIPPED, WILL KILL GOD'S TWO WITNESSES.

The Antichrist is not the only one who will have miraculous power. As we have already seen, the Two Witnesses of God will use all kinds of miracles both to preach Christ and to judge the world. They will have the power to kill their enemies with fire, prevent rainfall, turn water to blood and bring plagues on the earth as often as they wish. Their frequent use of these powers will create havoc on the world. The Two Witnesses will be hated by tens of millions of people who do not know God and are terrified by the judgments.

The Two Witnesses will be invincible for three and one-half years. But after their work is finished, God will permit the Antichrist to kill them. The Apostle John in his vision speaks of this in Revelation 11:7:

> Revelation 11:7 (NIV)
> *"Now when they have finished their testimony, the beast that comes up from the Abyss will attack them, and overpower and kill them."*

No doubt the Antichrist will be more popular than ever before. He will have been able to kill God's Two Witnesses. It will be a great time of rejoicing and praise to the Antichrist. The Apostle John tells us of this rejoicing in Revelation 11:8-10 —

Revelation 11:8-10 (NIV)

8) *"Their bodies will lie in the street of the great city, which is figuratively called Sodom and Egypt, where also their Lord was crucified.*

9) *For three and a half days men from every people, tribe, language and nation will gaze on their bodies and refuse them burial.*

10) *The inhabitants of the earth will gloat over them and will celebrate by sending each other gifts, because these two prophets had tormented those who live on the earth."*

According to Revelation 11:9, how long will the nations look at the prophets bodies lying in the street?

_____

_____

_____

_____

How do you think that the whole world will be able to see the two bodies lying in the street?

_____

_____

_____

_____

Why do you think that no one will be allowed to bury the dead bodies of the Two Witnesses?

_____

_____

_____

_____

According to Revelation 11:10, just how happy will the world be at the death of the Two Witnesses?

_____

_____

_____

_____

Evidently the Antichrist will not be satisfied with just killing God's Two Witnesses. The Bible tells us that he will display their bodies in the streets. Through worldwide television and other forms of mass communications, the world will be able to look at their corpses. Merely looking at the decaying bodies of these two men will not satisfy the people. They will declare a great holiday and send gifts to each other. Their leader, the Antichrist, will have proven his greatness by being resurrected from a fatal head wound. And at long last the Two Witnesses who will have haunted the world with their preaching and judgments will be dead. But at the very moment when the world is rejoicing in the death of God's two messengers, God Himself astounds the people. The Apostle John tells us what miracle God will do in Revelation 11:11-13 —

The Great Tribulation - Part Two

> Revelation 11:11-13 (NIV)
> *11) "But after the three and a half days a breath of life from God entered them, and they stood on their feet, and terror struck those who saw them.*
> *12) Then they heard a loud voice from heaven saying to them, 'Come up here.' And they went up to heaven in a cloud, while their enemies looked on.*
> *13) At that very hour there was a severe earthquake and a tenth of the city collapsed. Seven thousand people were killed in the earthquake, and the survivors were terrified and gave glory to the God of heaven."*

According to Revelation 11:11-13, what four things does God do that shows His mighty power to the world?

_____

_____

_____

According to Revelation 11:11-13, what will be the response of the people of the world to God's miraculous act?

_____

_____

_____

One can only imagine the impact of this great miracle. Tens of millions of people will be staring at the corpses of the Two Witnesses. Televisions around the world will be carrying this event as this new holiday continues. But suddenly these two feared men come back to life and rise to their feet. There will be a loud voice from heaven which will certainly be heard by millions. These Two Witnesses will ascend into heaven while the whole world looks on. Almost immediately after the Two Witnesses are gone, there will be an earthquake in Jerusalem. Almost a tenth of the city will be destroyed and 7,000 people will die. The world will be astounded at this miracle and know it was from God. Yet the masses, while acknowledging God's power, will soon forget Him. The Antichrist will step in and once again sway the hardened hearts of the people to follow him.

The Great Tribulation - Part Two

C. THE ANTICHRIST WILL DESTROY WORLDWIDE RELIGION.

The Antichrist will be much relieved to see that the Two Witnesses are gone. The Antichrist will sense his increasing power and will move to wipe out anything that stands in his way of world control. The greatest opposition still standing between the Antichrist and total worship will be Worldwide Religion. As we saw in the previous chapter, the Antichrist had made an unholy alliance with Worldwide False Religion. John tells us that during this alliance Worldwide Religion will dominate the Antichrist. The Antichrist will resent this dominance and turn against the 'prostitute,' known as 'Mystery Babylon.' In the prophecy he saw in heaven, John tells us what the Antichrist and his followers will do to the Worldwide False Religion in Revelation 17:15-17 —

Revelation 17:15-17 (NIV)
15) "Then the angel said to me, 'The waters you saw, where the prostitute sits, are peoples, multitudes, nations and languages.
16) The beast and the ten horns you saw will hate the prostitute. They will bring her to ruin and leave her naked; they will eat her flesh and burn her with fire.
17) For God has put it into their hearts to accomplish his purpose by agreeing to give the beast their power to rule, until God's words are fulfilled.'"

According to verse 16, how does the Antichrist feel about the 'prostitute?'

_____

_____

_____

The Great Tribulation - Part Two

According to Revelation 17:16, what will the Antichrist and his followers do to the 'prostitute?'

_____

_____

_____

_____

According to Revelation 17:17, who will give the Antichrist his desire and power to destroy False World Religion?

_____

_____

_____

_____

God hates false religion. He hates it when people take His truth and pervert it with lies. He hates it when lies about God are used to confuse people and lead them away from Him. God will allow the Antichrist to destroy the False Worldwide Religion. With this religious system gone, the Antichrist will be ready to set himself up as 'God' and demand the worship of the world.

D. THE ANTICHRIST BREAKS TREATY WITH ISRAEL AND SETS HIMSELF UP AS GOD.

The Antichrist will truly be amazing. Through his cleverness, brute force, and miraculous signs, he will rise to absolute power. With his world renowned power he will finally show his true intentions. The Bible tells us that the Antichrist will break his peace treaty with Israel and forcibly set up his worship in the Temple. Israelis, who will have been deceived by the Antichrist, will be powerless to stop this hideous crime against them. The prophet Daniel predicted that the Antichrist would break his treaty with Israel:

> Daniel 9:27 (NIV)
> *"He will confirm a covenant with many for one 'seven.' In the middle of the 'seven' he will put an end to sacrifice and offering. And on a wing of the temple he will set up an abomination that causes desolation, until the end that is decreed is poured out on him."*

The Great Tribulation - Part Two

What do you think Daniel means when he says, 'In the middle of the seven he will put an end to the sacrifice and offering?'

_____

_____

_____

_____

_____

The prophet Daniel predicted that the Antichrist will set up an 'abomination that causes desolation, until the end that is decreed is poured out on him.' What do you think this means?

_____

_____

_____

_____

_____

BEHOLD YOUR GOD!

The Great Tribulation - Part Two

6

Daniel tells us that something horrible will happen when the Antichrist sets up his kingdom in the Temple. So horrible is this act that Daniel calls it an 'abomination.' The word 'abomination' means 'evil beyond belief.' This act of absolute rebellion and rage towards God will cause the world to become desolate. Jesus talked about how awful this time will be when He said in Matthew 24:15-22 —

Matthew 24:15-22 (NIV)

15) "So when you see standing in the holy place 'the abomination that causes desolation,' spoken of through the prophet Daniel - let the reader understand-
16) then let those who are in Judea flee to the mountains.
17) Let no one on the roof of his house go down to take anything out of the house.
18) Let no one in the field go back to get his cloak.
19) How dreadful it will be in those days for pregnant women and nursing mothers! 20) Pray that your flight will not take place in the winter or on the Sabbath.
21) For then there will be great distress, unequaled from the beginning of the world until now and never to be equaled again.
22) If those days had not been cut short, no one would survive, but for the sake of the elect those days will be shortened."

At last the Antichrist will be free to do what he wants to do. The Antichrist will want to be worshipped as God. By now the lost masses will worship him. For a brief moment in time, the Antichrist will have reached his goal and will bask in the warmth of worldwide adoration. The Apostle Paul clearly predicted what the Antichrist will do at that time:

---

2 Thessalonians 2:4 (NIV)
"He will oppose and will exalt himself over everything that is called God or is worshipped, so that he sets himself up in God's temple, proclaiming himself to be God."

II. THE ANTICHRIST WILL HAVE THE SATANIC ASSISTANCE OF THE FALSE PROPHET.

By the second half of the Tribulation, the Antichrist will be at the peak of his power. Yet, he will still crave even more worship and want more control of the inhabitants of the earth. It is hard to imagine how difficult it will be for the Antichrist to get several billion people to worship him. John tells us that the Antichrist will have a helper who will assist him in taking over total control of the hearts, minds and lives of everyone. The book of Revelation tells us the Antichrist will have the assistance of the False Prophet (Revelation 19:20). John's vision tells us about this False Prophet in Revelation 13:11-18 —

Revelation 13:11-18 (NIV)

11) "Then I saw another beast, coming out of the earth. He had two horns like a lamb, but he spoke like a dragon.

12) He exercised all the authority of the first beast on his behalf, and made the earth and its inhabitants worship the first beast, whose fatal wound had been healed.

13) And he performed great and miraculous signs, even causing fire to come down from heaven to earth in full view of men.

14) Because of the signs he was given power to do on behalf of the first beast, he deceived the inhabitants of the earth. He ordered them to set up an image in honor of the beast who was wounded by the sword and yet lived.

15) He was given power to give breath to the image of the first beast, so that it could speak and cause all those who refused to worship the image to be killed.

16) He also forced everyone, small and great, rich and poor, free and slave, to receive a mark on his right hand or on his forehead,

17) so that no one could buy or sell unless he had the mark, which is the name of the beast or the number of his name.

18) This calls for wisdom. If anyone has insight, let him calculate the number of the beast, for it is man's number. His number is 666."

WHAT WILL BE THE FALSE PROPHET'S PLAN OF ACTIONS?

A. THE FALSE PROPHET WILL HAVE A POWERFULLY DECEPTIVE INFLUENCE ON THE WORLD.

Like the Antichrist, this False Prophet will be full of evil, deception, and lies. Outside of the Antichrist, he will be the most powerful person on the earth. The Apostle John wrote of him in Revelation 13:11-12 —

Revelation 13:11-12 (NIV)
11) "Then I saw another beast, coming out of the earth. He had two horns like a lamb, but he spoke like a dragon.
12) He exercised all the authority of the first beast on his behalf, and made the earth and its inhabitants worship the first beast, whose fatal wound had been healed."

In describing the False Prophet, John tells us that 'he had two horns like a lamb but spoke like a dragon.' What do you think that means?

_____

_____

_____

_____

The False Prophet will be very deceptive. He will come across as a very loving and harmless person, gentle like a lamb. But the words he will speak will be hateful and ferocious like a dragon. John tells us that he will have all the authority of the Antichrist. Yet he will only use that authority to honor the Antichrist and help him fulfill his dreams. The False Prophet will be driven by one goal. And that goal will be to make 'the earth and it's inhabitants worship the first beast.'

B.   THE FALSE PROPHET WILL HAVE INCREDIBLE POWER.

The False Prophet will have a tremendous job to do. His job will be to make all the people of the earth worship the Antichrist. Yet the False Prophet will be equipped for the job because he will be given incredible power. John tells us in Revelation 13:13-14a —

Revelation 13:13-14a (NIV)
13) "And he performed great and miraculous signs, even causing fire to come down from heaven to earth in full view of men.
14a) Because of the signs he was given power to do on behalf of the first beast, he deceived the inhabitants of the earth."

According to Revelation 13:13-14a, the False Prophet will be able to use his power two different ways. What are those ways?

_____

_____

_____

_____

The power of the False Prophet will be incredible. The whole world will be watching while he causes fire to come down from heaven to the earth. This and other great and miraculous signs that he performs will have the earth in awe of him. He will combine this great miraculous power with another awesome gift: the incredible skill to deceive the masses of the world. Like the Antichrist, he will fool tens of millions of people with what appears to be kind and loving words. But in the end this deceiver will work with the Antichrist to control and destroy most of mankind.

C. THE FALSE PROPHET WILL HAVE A PLAN TO CAPTURE THE WORLD'S WORSHIP.

To control the minds and actions of several billion people will be a most difficult task. No dictator in history has been able to accomplish such an incredible feat. The False Prophet under the orders of the Antichrist will be sent out to do what has been impossible in the past. John tells us that the False Prophet will use an idol or religious statue to awe the world.

Revelation 13:14b-15 (NIV)
14b) "He ordered them to set up an image in honor of the beast who was wounded by the sword and yet lived.
15) He was given power to give breath to the image of the first beast, so that it could speak and cause all who refused to worship the image to be killed."

In some way, the False Prophet will create an amazing idol or statue in Jerusalem. John tells us that this image will somehow be able to speak through the power of illusion or demonic influence. The world will be amazed at this great idol. But they will also be terrified: anyone who refuses to bow down and worship this idol will be killed. Every human being has a deeply spiritual side. The False Prophet will play on the religious yearnings and fear of the people so that they will rush to worship the statue of the Antichrist.

The Great Tribulation - Part Two | 6

D. THE FALSE PROPHET WILL HAVE AN ECONOMIC PLAN TO BRING THE WORLD TO ITS KNEES.

The False Prophet will clearly understand that if he can control a person's finances, he can control that person's life. Therefore, using the latest technology available, the world's economy will be controlled from one central place. The prophet John predicted that the Antichrist will have absolute control over everyone's finances. Through the False Prophet, he will control the world.

> Revelation 13:16-18 (NIV)
> 16) "He also forced everyone, small and great, rich and poor, free and slave, to receive a mark on his right hand or on his forehead,
> 17) so that no one could buy or sell unless he had the mark, which is the name of the beast or the number of his name.
> 18) This calls for wisdom. If anyone has insight, let him calculate the number of the beast, for it is man's number. His number is 666."

According to Revelation 13:16-18, everyone will have to wear a mark on his hand or forehead. What will that mark be?

_____

_____

_____

_____

According to Revelation 13:16, will anyone be excluded from having to receive the 'mark of the beast?'

_____

_____

_____

_____

According to Revelation 13:17, what will happen to those who do not have the 'mark of the beast.'

_____

_____

_____

_____

The pressure on the people of the world to worship the Antichrist will be incredible. Those who refuse to worship him will be murdered or starved to death. The False Prophet's plan to secure the worship of the Antichrist will be all but fail-proof. And so for a few brief moments in history, the Antichrist will secure the worship of most everyone.

CONCLUSION

As people enter the second half of the Tribulation the earth will be a frightening place. There will be awesome miracles, intrigue, plagues, death, and a ferocious world dictatorship. Step by step, little by little, the scene will be set for the final war of this earth and the Second Coming of Jesus Christ.

NOTES

7 | Armageddon and the Second Coming of Christ

At the end of the Tribulation, life will be unbearable. The Antichrist and his False Prophet will have moved into world control. With the Antichrist's opposition gone, he will seem destined to be the world's dictator for years to come. Yet God is the one who ultimately is in charge of the world. God is the one who sets the times of history. While it will appear that the Antichrist is in charge, God will quickly bring history to its close. He will do so with incredible judgments, a massive war, and the Second Coming of Jesus Christ.

> ## IN THIS CHAPTER, WE WILL DISCUSS THE AWESOME EVENTS THAT USHER IN THE SECOND COMING OF JESUS CHRIST.

Armageddon and the Second Coming of Christ

Armageddon and the Second Coming of Christ

I. THE SECOND COMING OF CHRIST WILL OCCUR AFTER INCREDIBLE JUDGMENTS ARE POURED OUT ON THE EARTH.

The Tribulation will be the most terrible period in the history of the world. During this time Satan will be unleashing his power through the Antichrist. Mankind will rebel against God like never before. But there will be something else that will cause this time to appear to be like 'hell on earth.' God Himself will pour out judgments on the world for its rebellion.

A. GOD WILL ALLOW THE WORLD TO ENDURE INCREDIBLE JUDGMENTS.

The Bible tells us that throughout the Tribulation there will be judgments and suffering like the world has never seen before. The book of Revelation speaks of terrible things happening. Here is a partial list of some of these judgments:

- Wars & Famines — Revelation 6:3-5
- Inflation Out of Control — Revelation 6:6
- Multiple Earthquakes — Revelation 6:12-17
- Because of the Wars, Famines & Earthquakes — at Least Half of World's Population Dies — Revelation 6:7-8; 9:13
- Horrible & Incurable Plagues — Luke 21:11
- The Killing of Millions of Christians — Revelation 6:9-11
- Stars & Meteors Crash into the Earth — Revelation 6:12-14
- Mountains Crumbling Down — Revelation 6:14
- Wild Stinging Locusts — Revelation 9:3-6

Armageddon and the Second Coming of Christ

Jesus predicted that the suffering of the world in the Tribulation would be worse than anything we could imagine. He said in Matthew 24:21-22 —

Matthew 24:21-22 (NCV)
21) "Because at that time there will be much trouble. There will be more trouble than there has ever been since the beginning of the world until now, and nothing as bad will ever happen again.
22) God has decided to make that terrible time short. Otherwise, no one would go on living. But God will make that time short to help the people He has chosen."

B. SUFFERING WILL BE AT AN ALL TIME HIGH AT THE END OF THE TRIBULATION.

It would appear that the horrible wrath of God upon the world will intensify as the Battle of Armageddon and the Return of Christ draw near. In Revelation 16, John saw a vision of God's wrath being poured out on the earth. What he describes is truly horrible. Yet some of these judgments and Satan's response to them will prepare the world for the great Battle of Armageddon.

The Bible tells us that at the end of the Tribulation, angels will be pouring destruction on the earth. Horrible things will happen on the earth due to the work of these angels. These judgments include:

- Every person who has the mark of the Beast will be given painful sores (Revelation 16:2).
- The ocean will be turned to blood and everything in the sea will die (Revelation 16:3).
- The rivers and all sources of water will turn into blood (Revelation 16:4).
- The sun will intensify in heat, scorching those on earth (Revelation 16:8-9).
- The world will be covered in darkness causing people to gnaw on their tongues in agony, while cursing God (Revelation 16:10-11).

Armageddon and the Second Coming of Christ

The plagues that God will send at the end of the Tribulation will be horrifying. But John tells us that two other amazing things will take place as God curses the rebellious earth. He said in Revelation 16:12 —

Revelation 16:12 (NIV)
"The sixth angel poured out his bowl on the great river Euphrates, and its water was dried up to prepare the way for the kings from the East."

According to Revelation 16:12, what will happen to the 'great river Euphrates?'

_____

_____

_____

_____

Why will it be important that the 'great river Euphrates' drys up?

_____

_____

_____

_____

Armageddon and the Second Coming of Christ

The Bible tells us that in the final war all the kingdoms of the world will come together to fight in the great Battle of Armageddon. There is a mighty barrier, called the Euphrates River, separating the Far East kingdoms such as China, Japan, India, etc. from marching against Israel. The great river Euphrates is 1,700 miles long, stretching from Turkey to the Persian Gulf. God, by drying up the Euphrates, will prepare a way for the mighty millions of the Far East to descend on Israel.

John tells us in Revelation 16:13 that he saw a vision of something else happening that was truly amazing. He tells us in Revelation 16:13-16 —

Revelation 16:13-16 (NIV)

13) "Then I saw three evil spirits that looked like frogs; they came out of the mouth of the dragon, out of the mouth of the beast and out of the mouth of the false prophet.

14) They are spirits of demons performing miraculous signs, and they go out to the kings of the whole world, to gather them for the battle on the great day of God Almighty.

15) Behold, I come like a thief! Blessed is he who stays awake and keeps his clothes with him, so that he may not go naked and be shamefully exposed.

16) Then they gathered together the kings to the place that in Hebrew is called Armageddon."

According to Revelation 16:13, who sends out these evil spirits that look like frogs?

_____

_____

_____

_____

According to Revelation 16:14, what two jobs will these demons have?

_____

_____

_____

_____

Satan, moving through demonic beings, will call in the great armies of the world to wipe out Israel once and for all. Satan, in his delusion and confusion, will think that if he can destroy Israel, he can destroy God. Therefore, preparations for the battle of Armageddon will be set.

Armageddon and the Second Coming of Christ | 7

II. THE SECOND COMING OF JESUS CHRIST WILL NOT OCCUR BEFORE THE BATTLE OF ARMAGEDDON.

For two thousand years the Battle of Armageddon has been discussed by millions of people all over the world. The great Battle of Armageddon will bring together all the major armies of the world in one ferocious climactic combat. It will be the most deadly battle ever known in the history of the world. All the combined horrors of all the battles ever fought will not begin to compare with the death and destruction caused by this mighty conflict. The Bible tells us that it will be the final battle that ushers in the Return of Jesus Christ.

A.   WHERE IS ARMAGEDDON?

The Bible specifically tells us where the final battle will be fought. It should be no surprise to us that this great battle will be fought in Israel — involving God's chosen people — the Jews.

> Revelation 16:16 (NIV)
> *"Then they gathered the kings together to the place that in Hebrew is called Armageddon."*

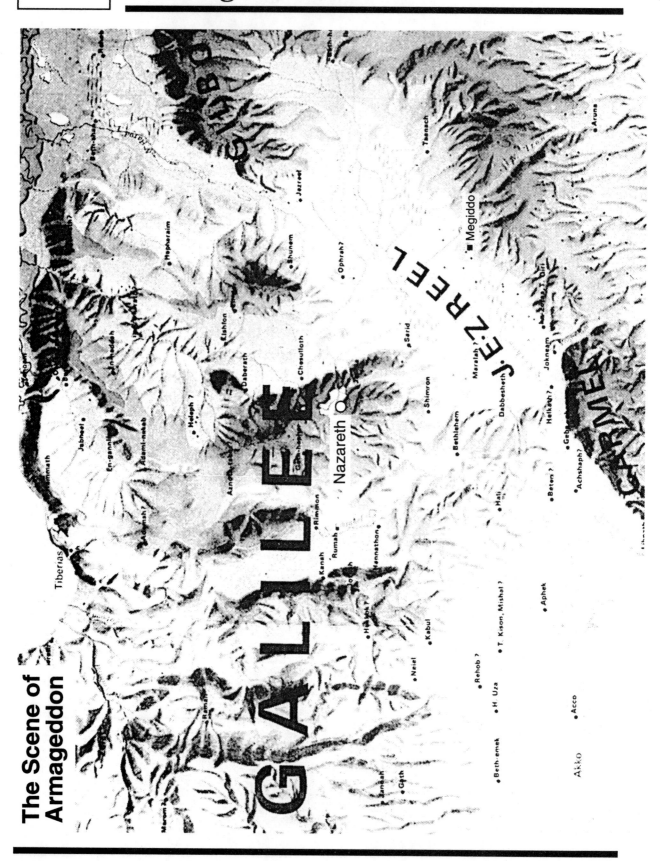

The Scene of Armageddon

Armageddon and the Second Coming of Christ

Armageddon is located near a small mountain by the Mediterranean Sea called Mount Megiddo. This mountain overlooks a valley that stretches out to the east. It is a valley that is 14 miles wide and 20 miles long. The Bible tells us that this famous valley will be the center point of the greatest war ever fought. The valley of Armageddon is a strategic place. It is one of the most important crossroads in Palestine. Napoleon, one of the greatest military leaders of all time, once stated that apart from Armageddon, perhaps there is no other location in the world where the armies of the world could gather for a mighty war.

B.   WHO WILL MARCH INTO ISRAEL FOR THIS FINAL BATTLE?

At the end of the Tribulation, the world will find itself amassing its armies to descend upon Israel for a final battle. Satan, using powerful demons, will call hundreds of millions of soldiers to come from all over the world. It will be Satan's goal to wipe out the Jews and take a major stand against God. There will be another reason why the armies of the world will ascend on Israel. Many of the nations will be sending their armies to confront the Antichrist.

The Antichrist will have promised the world peace and prosperity. But he will not be able to fulfill his promises. Instead, the nations will have to endure one horrible crisis after another. Finally, large segments of this world will turn against the Antichrist. They will march on the Middle East to have a final brutal battle for world power. Israel will be the focal point of that power. The prophet Daniel foretold this incredible encounter of the world's forces:

> Daniel 11:40-44 (NIV)
> *40) "At the time of the end the king of the South will engage him in battle, and the king of the North will storm out against him with chariots and cavalry and a great fleet of ships. He will invade many countries and sweep through them like a flood.*
> *41) He will also invade the Beautiful Land. Many countries will fall, but Edom, Moab and the leaders of Ammon will be delivered from his hand.*
> *42) He will extend his power over many countries; Egypt, will not escape.*
> *43) He will gain control of the treasures of gold and silver and all the riches of Egypt, with the Libyans and Nubians in submission.*
> *44) But reports from the east and the north will alarm him, and he will set out in a great rage to destroy and annihilate many."*

In Daniel 11 the prophet predicts that the nations of the South and North will converge on Israel.

Who do you think these nations of the South are?

_____

_____

_____

_____

The nations of the South (south of Palestine) would include the Arab states and the vast continent of Africa. These nations combining their strength will be able to amass an army probably numbering in the millions.

Armageddon and the Second Coming of Christ

7

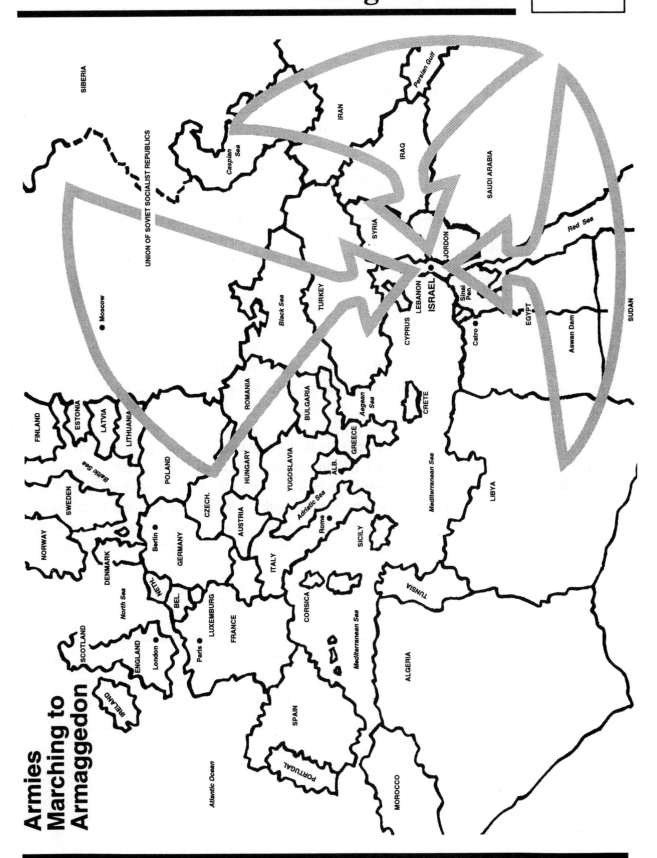

Armies Marching to Armaggedon

Armageddon and the Second Coming of Christ

Daniel also speaks of the kings from the North.

Who do you think these nations of the North are?

_____

_____

_____

_____

The nations of the North (north of Palestine) would include the armies of Russia and troops sent by Eastern Europe including such countries as Poland, Ukraine, Lithuania and Latvia.

In Daniel 11:40-43, the Bible tells us that the Antichrist and his western alliance will seem to have the upper hand in the first phase of the conflict. It would appear that the Antichrist with his brilliant military skills is able to hold off the North and do even better against the countries of the South. Perhaps for a small time during this conflict the Antichrist will be somewhat confident that he will continue to rule the world. However, he will hear some very disturbing news. Daniel tells us what that bad news will be:

> Daniel 11:44 (NIV)
> *"But reports from the east and the north will alarm him, and he will set out in a great rage to destroy and annihilate many."*

Armageddon and the Second Coming of Christ

Daniel tells us that the Antichrist will have to face the greatest military challenge ever. Somehow the nations of the North will rebound and advance once again towards the Antichrist. But even worse than that will be the news that an army of 200 million from the East is advancing towards him for war (see Revelation 9:14-16). The stage will be set for the greatest warfare of all time. The great Battle of Armageddon will include hundreds of millions of men. It will be a war that the Antichrist will not win.

C. COULD THE WORLD'S GREATEST NIGHTMARE BE ANY WORSE THAN THE BATTLE OF ARMAGEDDON?

The world has never witnessed anything close to the death and destruction that will occur at the Battle of Armageddon. As the armies of the East march on Jerusalem, a third of the world's population will be slaughtered (see Revelation 9:14-16). There will be so much bloodshed in the battle itself that the Bible tells us there will be blood up to the horse's bridles.

> Revelation 14:20 (NIV)
> *"They were trampled in the winepress outside the city, and blood flowed out of the press, rising as high as the horses' bridles for a distance of 1,600 stadia."*

In the midst of the war, God will furiously send further wrath on a rebellious and decadent world. The apostle John tells us:

Armageddon and the Second Coming of Christ

Revelation 16:17-21 (NIV)
17) "The seventh angel poured out his bowl into the air, and out of the temple came a loud voice from the throne, saying, 'It is done!'
18) Then there came flashes of lightning, rumblings, peals of thunder and a severe earthquake. No earthquake like it has ever occurred since man has been on earth, so tremendous was the quake.
19) The great city split into three parts, and the cities of the nations collapsed. God remembered Babylon the Great and gave her the cup filled with the wine of the fury of his wrath.
20) Every island fled away and the mountains could not be found.
21) From the sky huge hailstones of about a hundred pounds each fell upon men. And they cursed God on account of the plague of hail, because the plague was so terrible."

According to Revelation 16:17-21, why do you think this will be one of the worst judgements on the earth?

_____

_____

_____

_____

We have here a rebellious world of people who will be literally slaughtering each other. At the Battle of Armageddon, the world will think that nothing worse could happen to it. They will be slaughtering each other as God's fury and judgment rains upon them. But something worse than even these events will befall them. The Bible tells us that Jesus Christ will appear in Person to destroy all the armies of the world.

III. JESUS CHRIST WILL APPEAR AND END THE BATTLE OF ARMAGEDDON.

Only Jesus Christ will be able to end the Battle of Armageddon. If He did not come back to end the war, then everyone would be annihilated (Matthew 24:21-22). The Bible says that just as Christ prepares to return, the world will shudder again under the weight of God's incredible judgments (Revelation 16:17-21). But at just the right moment Christ will return to this earth (Acts 3:19-21) just as He predicted in Matthew 24:30. The prophet John also saw a vision of the Second Coming of Christ. He describes for us this truly incredible moment in history. He said:

Revelation 19:11-21 (NIV)

11) "I saw heaven standing open and there before me was a white horse, whose rider is called Faithful and True. With justice he judges and makes war.

12) His eyes are like blazing fire, and on his head are many crowns. He has a name written on him that no one knows but he himself.

13) He is dressed in a robe dipped in blood, and his name is the Word of God.

14) The armies of heaven were following him, riding on white horses and dressed in fine linen, white and clean.

15) Out of his mouth comes a sharp sword with which to strike down the nations. 'He will rule them with an iron scepter.' He treads the winepress of the fury of the wrath of God Almighty.

---

7 Armageddon and the Second Coming of Christ

> Revelation 19:11-21 (NIV)
>
> *16) On his robe and on his thigh he has this name written: KING OF KINGS AND LORD OF LORDS.*
>
> *17) And I saw an angel standing in the sun, who cried in a loud voice to all the birds flying in midair, 'Come, gather together for the great supper of God,*
>
> *18) so that you may eat the flesh of kings, generals, and mighty men, of horses and their riders, and the flesh of all people, free and slave, small and great.*
>
> *19) Then I saw the beast and the kings of the earth and their armies gather together to make war against the rider on the horse and his army.*
>
> *20) But the beast was captured, and with him the false prophet who had performed the miraculous signs of his behalf. With these signs he had deluded those who had received the mark of the beast and worshipped his image. The two of them were thrown alive into the fiery lake of burning sulfur.*
>
> *21) The rest of them were killed with the sword that came out of the mouth of the rider on the horse, and all the birds gorged themselves on their flesh. "*

Using Revelation 19:11-12, describe as best you can how Christ will look at the Second Coming.

_____

_____

_____

_____

Armageddon and the Second Coming of Christ

KING of KINGS

7 | Armageddon and the Second Coming of Christ

According to Revelation 19:14, who do you think the armies of heaven will be?

_____

_____

_____

_____

John tells us in Revelation 19:19 that the armies of the world make a terrible mistake as Christ returns. What is that mistake?

_____

_____

_____

_____

According to Revelation 19:20, what happens to the Antichrist and the False Prophet?

_____

_____

_____

_____

Armageddon and the Second Coming of Christ | 7

According to Revelation 19:21, what happens to the soldiers at the Battle of Armageddon?

_____

_____

_____

_____

The greatest warrior that has been or will ever be is Jesus Christ. He will return to this world riding a white horse with all the armies of heaven following Him. He is not dependent upon the armies of heaven to fight for Him. He personally will destroy the world and the Antichrist with the brilliance of His splendor. The apostle Paul tells us in 2 Thessalonians 2:8 —

> 2 Thessalonians 2:8 (NIV)
> *"And then the lawless one will be revealed, whom the Lord Jesus will overthrow with the breath of his mouth and destroy by the splendor of his coming."*

The day that Christ returns will be a day like no other. No one will be able to escape Him as He returns to earth to rule from Jerusalem for a thousand years. The prophet Zechariah speaks of His coming and tells of some of the events that will occur on that day:

7 | Armageddon and the Second Coming of Christ

Zechariah 14:4-7; 9 (NIV)

4) "On that day his feet will stand on the Mount of Olives, east of Jerusalem, and the Mount of Olives will be split in two from east to west, forming a great valley, with half of the mountain moving north and half moving south.

5) You will flee by my mountain valley, for it will extend to Azel. You will flee as you fled from the earthquake in the days of Uzziah king of Judah. Then the Lord my God will come, and all the holy ones with him.

6) On that day there will be no light, no cold or frost.

7) It will be a unique day, without daytime or nighttime - a day known to the Lord. When evening comes, there will be light.

9) The Lord will be king over the whole earth. On that day there will be one Lord, and his name the only name."

What a day it will be as Jesus Christ returns to defeat evil and set up His thousand year reign on this earth. What a joy it will be for those of us who know Christ to rule with Him and to enjoy this planet in a whole new way (Revelation 20:4). What a time it will be as we get ready to spend an eternity in Heaven with Jesus Christ.

Armageddon and the Second Coming of Christ

IN CONCLUSION

It is truly amazing to understand how our world will end. The Bible tells us that in the end Jesus Christ will rule triumphant over all evil. After studying these incredible events of the end times we are left asking three questions:

1. When will Christ Return?

Of course no one knows. Maybe today. Maybe tomorrow. Maybe next year. But this much we do know — that Christ will come even as people on this earth mock us for believing in Him. The Bible speaks of this in 2 Peter 3 —

---

2 Peter 3:3-4; 8-10a (TLB)

3) "First, I want to remind you that in the last days there will come scoffers who will do every wrong they can think of and laugh at the truth.
4) This will be their line of argument: 'So Jesus promised to come back, did he? Then where is he? He'll never come! Why, as far back as anyone can remember, everything has remained exactly as it was since the first day of creation...'
8) But don't forget this, dear friends, that a day or a thousand years from now is like tomorrow to the Lord.
9) He isn't really being slow about his promised return, even though it sometimes seems that way. But he is waiting, for the good reason that he is not willing that any should perish, and he is giving more time for sinners to repent.
10) The day of the Lord is surely coming, as unexpectedly as a thief."

2. If Christ were to Return Today — Would I be Ashamed?

The apostle John, to whom God gave so many visions about the end times, made a simple challenge to all those who wait for the return of Christ. He said:

> 1 John 2:28 (NIV)
> *"And now, dear children, continue in him, so that when he appears we may be confident and unashamed before him at his coming."*

Are we who are Christians living in such a way that we won't be ashamed of ourselves when Christ comes back? How are we different from the world around us in our speech, our actions, and our attitudes?

3. What Must I do to Get Ready for the Return of Christ?

The apostle John, moved along by the Holy Spirit, spoke both to those who know Christ and those who don't know Him. In order to be ready for Christ's return, John invites us to 'take the free gift of the water of life' which is Christ. He said in Revelation 22:17 —

> Revelation 22:17 (NIV)
> *"The Spirit and the bride say, 'Come!' And let him who hears say, 'Come!' Whoever is thirsty, let him come; and whoever wishes, let him take the free gift of the water of life. "*

Armageddon and the Second Coming of Christ

All of God's prophecies will come to pass. Jesus Christ will return to this earth; He will return in the air for His church. Will He take you with Him to heaven? Do you know beyond the shadow of a doubt that if Christ appeared this very moment, your eternal destiny would be heaven? If you are unsure, here is a simple prayer you can pray:

> **LORD JESUS, I KNOW THAT I DESERVE THE WRATH YOU WILL BE BRINGING ON THE EARTH. BUT I THANK YOU THAT YOU LOVE ME AND DIED TO PAY THE FULL PENALTY FOR MY SIN. I ACCEPT THE FREE GIFT OF SALVATION YOU OFFER, AND I TURN AWAY FROM MY SIN AND INVITE YOU TO TAKE YOUR RIGHTFUL PLACE AS MY LORD AND SAVIOR. THANK YOU FOR GIVING ME YOUR ETERNAL LIFE**

The closing verses of the Bible encourages us with a word from Jesus Christ, and reminds us that in the meantime, God is watching out for us:

Revelation 22:20-21 (NIV)
20) "He who testifies to these things says, 'Yes, I am coming soon.' Amen. Come, Lord Jesus.
21) The grace of the Lord Jesus be with God's people. Amen."

Armageddon and the Second Coming of Christ

NOTES

_____

_____

_____

_____

_____

_____

_____

_____

_____

_____

_____

_____

_____

_____

_____

_____

_____

_____

Bibliography

Dyer, Charles H. *World News and Bible Prophecy*. Wheaton: Tyndale House Publishers, 1993.

Feinberg, Charles L. *Focus on Prophecy*. Westwood, New Jersey: Fleming H. Revell Co., 1964.

Feinberg, Charles L. *The Prophecy of Ezekiel*. Chicago: Moody Press, 1969.

France, R.T. *Tyndale New Testament Commentaries: Matthew*. Grand Rapids: W.B. Eerdmans Publishing Co., 1985.

Goldingay, John E. *Word Biblical Commentary: Daniel*. Dallas: Word Publishing Co., 1989.

Graham, Billy. *Storm Warning*. Dallas: Word Publishing Co., 1992.

Jeffery, Grant R. *Messiah: War in the Middle East & the Road to Armageddon*. New York: Bantam Books, 1992.

Jeremiah, David. *Escape the Coming Night*. Dallas: Word Publishing Co., 1990.

Jeremiah, David. *The Handwriting on the Wall*. Dallas: Word Publishing Co., 1992.

LaHaye, Tim. *No Fear of the Storm*. Sisters, Oregon: Multnomah Press, 1992.

Morris, Leon. *Tyndale New Testament Commentaries: 1 and 2 Thessalonians (revised)*. Grand Rapids: W.B. Eerdmans Publishing Co., 1984.

Morris, Leon. *Tyndale New Testament Commentaries: Revelation (revised)*. Grand Rapids: W.B. Eerdmans Publishing Co., 1987.

Mounce, Robert H. *What Are We Waiting For? A Commentary on Revelation*. Grand Rapids: W.B. Eerdmans Publishing Co., 1992.

Pache, René. *The Return of Jesus Christ* translated by William S. LaSor. Chicago: Moody Press, 1955.

Pentecost, J. Dwight. *Prophecy for Today* (revised). Grand Rapids: Discovery House Publishers, 1989.

Pentecost, J. Dwight. *Things To Come*. Grand Rapids: Zondervan Publishing House, 1958.

Pentecost, J. Dwight. *Will Man Survive?* Grand Rapids: Zondervan Publishing House, 1990.

Reiter, Richard R. *The Rapture: Pre-, Mid-, or Post- Tribulational?* Grand Rapids: Zondervan Publishing House, 1984.

Ryrie, Charles C. *Basic Theology.* Wheaton: Victor Books, 1982.

Sauer, Erich. *The Triumph of the Crucified* translated by G.H. Lang. Grand Rapids: W.B. Eerdmans Publishing Co., 1957.

Stedman, Ray C. *God's Final Word.* Grand Rapids: Discovery House Publishers, 1991.

Tan, Paul L. *Encyclopedia of 7700 Illustrations: Signs of the Times.* Rockville, Maryland: Assurance Publishers, 1979.

Tan, Paul L. *Jesus Is Coming.* Rockville, Maryland: Assurance Publishers, 1982.

Walvoord, John F. *Armageddon, Oil, and the Middle East Crisis* (revised). Grand Rapids: Zondervan Publishing House, 1990.

Walvoord, John F. (ed.) *Chafer's Systematic Theology, Volume Two.* Wheaton: Victor Books, 1988.

Walvoord, John F. *Daniel: The Key to Prophetic Revelation.* Chicago: Moody Press, 1971.

Walvoord, John F. *Major Bible Prophecies.* Grand Rapids: Zondervan Publishing House, 1991.

Walvoord, John F. *Prophecy.* Nashville: Thomas Nelson Publishers, 1993.

Walvoord, John F. *The Rapture Question.* Grand Rapids: Zondervan Publishing House, 1957.

Walvoord, John F. *The Revelation of Jesus Christ.* Chicago: Moody Press, 1966.

White, John Wesley. *Thinking the Unthinkable.* Lake Mary, Florida: Creation House Publishers, 1992.

Wiersbe, Warren W. *Be Ready: 1 & 2 Thessalonians.* Wheaton: Victor Books, 1979.

Wood, Leon J. *The Bible and Future Events.* Grand Rapids: Zondervan Publishing House, 1973.

Wright, John W. (ed.) *The Universal Almanac 1993.* Kansas City: Andrews and McMeel, 1992.

About Shepherd Ministries

Shepherd Ministries is a comprehensive youth resource organization, meeting the needs of the American teenager through national conferences, weekly talk-radio, book publishing, video productions, music recordings and a monthly youth magazine.

•**Dawson McAllister Student Conferences-** The backbone of Shepherd Ministries is the weekend conferences around which the organization began. These weekend conferences are held around the country, changing the lives of tens of thousands of students through the ministry of music and praise from Todd Proctor and Joel Engle, the illusion and comedy of Mark Matlock, and the dynamic teaching of Dawson McAllister.

•**Dawson McAllister LIVE!-** Shepherd Ministries' weekly radio talk show brings troubled, confused and hurting teenagers into contact with straight talk and clear Biblical guidance. Each student that calls and receives Dawson's compassionate counsel on the air represents thousands of others with similar problems.

•**Youth Resource Products-** Shepherd Ministries publishes student manuals and produces video series by premiere youth communicator Dawson McAllister. His direct application of Biblical principles to the issues facing teens today is refreshing and so needed in reaching out to America's teens in the nineties.

•**Teen Quest Magazine-** Reaching kids wherever they are is the goal of **TQ**, Shepherd's monthly teen magazine. With interviews of prominent Christian artists, topical articles dealing with the tough issues of the day and many other exciting features, **TQ** is designed to minister to today's Christian teen.

FOR MORE INFORMATION ABOUT ANY OF SHEPHERD'S AREAS OF MINISTRY, PLEASE CALL US AT (214) 570-7599.

More From Dawson McAllister and Shepherd Ministries...

STUDENT MANUALS FROM DAWSON
A Walk With Christ To The Cross
A Walk With Christ Through The Resurrection
Discussion Manual For Student Relationships Vols. I, II, III
Discussion Manual For Student Discipleship Vols. I, II
Pack Your Bags: Jesus Is Coming
Student Conference Follow-up Manual
Search For Significance
Student Conference Follow-up Manual
The Great War
Who Are You, God?
Who Are You, Jesus?
You, God, And Your Sexuality

TEACHER MANUALS FROM DAWSON
A Walk With Christ To The Cross
Discussion Manual For Student Relationships Vols. I, II, III
Pack Your Bags: Jesus Is Coming
Preparing Your Teenager For Sexuality
The Great War
Who Are You, God?
Who Are You, Jesus?

BOOKS FROM DAWSON
Please Don't Tell My Parents: Answers For Kids In Crises

VIDEOS FROM DAWSON
A Walk With Christ To The Cross
Even The Lone Ranger Had Tonto: Friends
God Is Not Impressed With Joe Popular: Peer Pressure
How Far Is Too Far: Sex
Life 101- Learning To Say Yes! To Life
Looking For Life In All The Wrong Places: Worldliness
Preparing Your Teenager For Sexuality
When Tragedy Strikes
Why R.U.? - The Why and Way Out of Substance Abuse

MUSIC FROM SHEPHERD
One Day - Joel Engle
One Day: Praise And Worship Kit - Joel Engle
The Father I Never Had - Joel Engle
Everything Under The Son - Todd Proctor
Power Up: Praise For Youth - Todd Proctor
Power Up: Praise And Worship Kit - Todd Proctor
We Stand As One - Todd Proctor
We Stand As One: Praise and Worship Kit - Todd Proctor

OTHER SHEPHERD MINISTRIES PRODUCTS
Youth Worker's Fun Kit, Vol. I - Mark Matlock
A Safe Place - Jan Morrison
Brand Name Christians - Mike Worley
Cartoon Clip-Art For Youth Leaders Vols. I, II - Ron Wheele
Search For Significance - Robert McGee

• •

_____ **YES!** Please Send Me a *FREE* copy of your latest product catalog.

☐ STUDENT ☐ ADULT

Name_____

Church_____

Street Address_____

City/State/Zip_____

Phone Number_____

**For More Information Or To Order
Any Of These Products Contact:
Shepherd Ministries
2845 W. Airport Frwy. / Suite 137
Irving, TX.   75062
(214) 570-7599
FAX (214) 257-0632**